In late autumn 2017 I was sitting at home and
Somerset soldiers who had died during World War One (I have nearly 13,000
written, although I don't really know what to do with them), when the doorbell
rang. Feeling the need for a break and a cup of tea I went downstairs to see who was
calling.

I opened the door and, to my surprise, an old friend of mine had suddenly
popped up. Ava wanted to buy a book (*20 Mendip Pub Walks*) that I had published
some years ago. She was going to show it to her friends and then take the walks
with them. I explained to her that I held no copies, and that they were written such
a long time ago I did not even know if Amazon had them in stock. The
disappointment in her eyes was evident, and so she left, empty handed.

After I had finished my cup of tea I resolved to take a break from my historical
research. As a diversion I decided to write a series of walks that predominantly
featured South Somerset and it's Dorset border area. The resulting book of 20 walks
is dedicated my friend and I have named it *Perambulating with Ava* (this vivacious
lady also runs one of the best kept secrets in Yeovil, a restaurant named *My
Caribbean Corner* which can be found in Union Street, Yeovil (for SatNav use BA20
1PQ). A large public car-park is located just around the corner from it. For more
details you will need to log on and go to www.facebook.com/mycaribbeancorner
(retrieved from the internet 1st February 2018).

Although the walks I have written invariably feature a public house, please
remember that in these times, sadly, some pubs can, and do, suddenly disappear. At
the time of writing, they all existed. Also, from time to time, footpaths are
diverted/deleted, but once again, at the time of writing, they were all there.

Each walk also contains a Satellite Navigation Post Code, but there can be a small
difference in location between the type and brand of SatNav that you use. Despite
this, the ones I have used should put you on or near to the position of the start of the
walk.

Ava, I hope that you and your friends enjoy these perambulations.

Nether Compton, Dorset –
Sir Walter Raleigh's Potato Cave.

Distance: approximately 3.3 kilometres.
Time: 50 minutes.

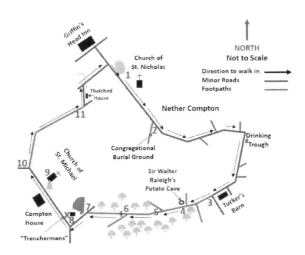

Nether Compton (population about 334) is a small village that that can be found some 2 kilometres north of the A30 between Yeovil and Sherborne.

Drive to the village of Nether Compton, near Sherborne, Dorset, and "park pretty me dear" near the village green (Grid Reference ST 597 173 and Global Positioning System co-ordinates 50° 57' 13.42" North, 2° 34' 26.00" West. For SatNav, use DT9 4QA. This pleasant walk is along public footpaths, bridleways and a minor Class C road. It is mostly on level ground and generally missed by the rambling population. It takes in some very pretty landscapes and a mysterious cave. The walk starts at a height of 42 metres above sea level, and at its lowest point is at 36 metres. The highest point of the walk reaches 82 metres.

W alk along the (1) road and keep the Church of St. Nicholas to your left. There are plenty of beautiful old houses in this village, some with Wisteria roaming along the walls and others with roses nestling in an old-fashioned way around the front doors.

Opposite the village hall you will find an old house ("Sherriff's Lodge") that was built in the Tudor style during 1890. In its front garden is an old metal pump that once served a well and it can still quite clearly be seen, although it is so obvious it can just as easily be missed.

Keep walking along the road and, almost opposite the "Old Forge" house you will find a walled Congregational Burial Ground (2) complete with a magnificent wooden panelled entrance. This walled burial ground is a Grade II building. It was first listed on the 11th July 1951 by Historic England; Source ID: 1154091 and English Heritage Legacy ID: 105616.

Regrettably vandalism took place even in those bygone days, and if you look carefully on some of the flatter pieces of the remaining wall you can make out where people carved their initials and the year of doing so. The earliest one I noted was dated 1771. This piece of stone facing now clings precariously to the wall, and sadly it will probably not last for very much longer.

This was caused by the stones being incorrectly cut against the grain, but the man who built the wall and gate, a certain London Merchant and Whig politician named John "Vulture" Hopkins, was not to know that (or did he, for he was known to be a bit of a sharp operator in those days?).

Walk on and where the road turns fiercely to the right, and in front of the house named "Quest", you will find a covered ham-stone drinking trough that is now filled with earth. A little further on you will find a recess in the wall where a spring is active.

Next you will come across a group of houses on your left known as Tucker's Barn. Opposite these buildings and just before a large Yew tree, (3) turn sharp right and walk up the bridleway. After 100 metres, another track joins from the left. Ignore this and walk straight ahead, going downhill. Here comes the first surprise.

A track joins from the right, and just at this track junction you will find metal gates that bar the entrance to a cave that has been hand-carved (4) into the soft sandstone. Local legend has it that it was here that Sir Walter Raleigh, (who lived in nearby Sherborne Castle), stored the first potatoes that he had brought back from America. Sadly, this is probably just urban myth, as the first potatoes were introduced into Europe by the Spanish some years earlier. It does make a nice story, for after all, it would make a very good place (cool and dark), to store potatoes.

Carry on a little way further down the hill and the track forks to the right. Ignore this and keep going straight ahead (5) and start walking uphill.

Where the track once again veers left, and beneath a magnificent example of a Scots Pine tree, walk through the metal gate immediately to your front (6) and follow the track along, keeping the mixed forest on your right. Ignore any paths that go to the left or right.

Keep walking along this track, going up-hill. Look out, depending on the time of year, for wild red currants, gooseberries, strawberries and blackberries. Large bunches of yellow wild primroses flourish, punctuated by the stringent and unmistakeable garlic smell of the wild Ramson with its distinctive white flowers.

The track now goes steeply downhill and joins a metalled track. A little covered well stands on your right (7) but you need to turn left here, keeping the well behind you. A large private lake that abounds with wildlife lies just over the hedge and on your right.

Walk straight ahead and you will find to your right the old Manor House with two magnificent stone Gryphons (8) standing sentinel.

Just beyond that lies one of Dorset's best kept secrets, "Trenchermans." It is a veritable Aladdin's Cave for the gourmet with a large selection of foods and wines to suit the most discerning palate, and unusually so, you need to be a member to be able to buy any of their gastronomic delights. The web site (retrieved from the web 1st September 2017) is at www.trenchermans.com.

Walk up the gravel drive and on the right, in front of the old Compton House, stands the Church of St. Michael's (9) close to a huge Cedar of Lebanon. The tree trunk has a massive circumference of some 10 metres (33 feet). It is the nearer one to the house, which almost hides the second, to the east of it. This is a grand specimen of a Cupressus Macrocarpa (commonly known as the Monterey Cypress and native of Central California, America), and is supposedly the second biggest of its type in England (the largest, with a circumference of 11.25 metres, can be found in Beauport Park, Hastings, Suffolk).

Both trees in the churchyard were planted somewhere around 1830. The area in which the trees grow is now managed as a nature conservation area.

Walk on down to where the track turns sharply to your left. Go straight ahead (10) across the field and keep Compton House behind you. The hedge will be on your right. A footpath sign can be seen in the far distance.

Follow the well-defined track through a little copse by this sign, emerging out the other side through a small metal gate. Nether Compton lies before you. Cross the field, keeping the hedge on your right. Go over the stile (11) and turn immediately left, keeping the thatched cottage to your right.

Walk up the metalled road (Flax Lane) and out though the ham-stone entrance, turning right. Enter the village of Nether Compton and cross over the Ford, deceptively dry in the summer season. After about 300 metres you come to a 'T' junction in the road. To your left, and about 200 metres away, stands the "Griffins Head Inn," an old hostelry dated about 1599 and now a listed building. At the time of writing it did not appear to have a web-site to check opening times. Turn right at this junction and walk back to where you parked your car.

Sherborne, Dorset –
The Saucepan Walk.

Distance: approximately 2.7 kilometres.
Time: 45 minutes.

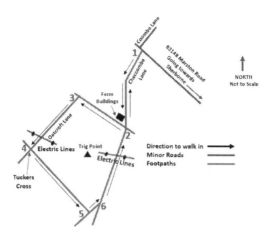

This pleasant short walk is along tracks and bridleways. There is a gentle uphill slope before the walk levels out at the top of the hill. I often used this area to exercise my daughter's Doberman dog, Merlin, should the weather have been a little inclement. I have named the walk The Saucepan Walk, and if you look at the map you will understand why. The old road that you will be walking along is no longer maintained and generally unsuitable for cars, but you may meet the occasional tractor and turfing vehicles. Hedges are growing either side of the walk and you can expect to see a great variety of wildlife, particularly butterflies.

You will find this location about 2½ kilometres north west of Sherborne, Dorset, and at Grid Reference ST 615 183, Global Positioning System co-ordinates 50° 57' 49.44" North, 2° 32' 53.43" West. For SatNav use DT9 4, Coombe Lane. The walk starts at about 135 metres and at its lowest point is 129 metres. Its highest point is near to 144 metres.

From Sherborne, pick up the B3148 (Marston Road) and drive towards Marston Magna. Follow the road out for about 1.5 kilometres. Drive up the gentle hill. The road will then start to go downhill. This is a fast stretch of road so slow down as you will need to keep your eyes open for a turning on the left with a clump

of three Beech Trees growing there. Coombe Lane is almost directly opposite the spot (1) where you will need to park.

Pull in to this old road *(marked by the red arrow)* and park safely. Leave plenty of space because tractors and turf lorry's regularly use what was once a tarmac road.

Walk up the gentle incline of the track (Checcombe Lane) and the first thing you will notice is the composition of the ground on your right-hand side. Erosion has revealed the stone from which this hill is made of.

After a little while you will come to some farm outbuildings on your right, with two radio aerials thrusting their way upwards. This track to your front is now crossed by a bridleway. Turn right (2) and follow it downhill, keeping the farm buildings on the right. Take the next left turning in the (3) track (Oatcroft Lane).

Walk along it until you pass beneath some overhead electric wires. About 70 metres later you will come to a cross-track. Take the turning to the left and walk along the well-defined lane. This crossing point is referred to locally as (4) 'Tuckers Cross'.

Walk on until you reach another track that passes in front of you. Take a left turn (5) and follow it along for about 100 metres. You then come to another not so well-defined bridleway (6) meeting the one that you are on. Ignore this and keep walking on ahead.

About 70 metres before the overhead electric wires cross in front of you there is a gap in the hedge on the left-hand side. A Trig Point near to the far electric pole marks the highest point of the hill at 149 metres.

Walk on and you will soon find yourself back to where you first turned right. Go straight ahead and back down the hill to your car.

Bradford Abbas, Dorset -
Roman Villas and All That.

Distance: approximately 4.6 kilometres.
Time: 1 hour.

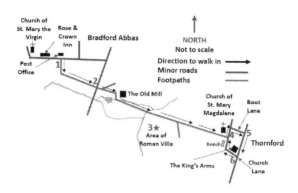

Bradford Abbas is a large village (population about 1,866) with Roman connections. If you are travelling from Yeovil, you will find the village about 1½ kilometres south of the main A30 road between Yeovil and Sherborne.

Find somewhere to park on the road near to the Post Office. It is located at Grid Reference ST 588 142, Global Positioning System co-ordinates 50° 55' 35.35" North, 2° 35' 12.34" West. For SatNav use DT9 6RF. The walk starts at approximately 38 metres above sea level, and at its lowest point is 34.5 metres. At its highest, the walk is about 61 metres.

O pposite the (1) Post Office (it lies quite close to the Rose and Crown public house), you will find a small footpath. Take this marked public footpath and follow it out through the kissing gate into the field beyond. Follow the well-trodden path that goes across this field to your left, leaving it by the kissing gate and out on to the tar macadam (2) road. The fast and shallow River Yeo flows beneath the stone bridge on your right.

Cross straight over the road, following the footpath sign. Take the right-hand track and head towards the group of buildings (The Old Mill) immediately to your front.

Turn right at the large house, keeping it on your left. Go through the kissing gate and over the stream and stone bridge into the next field, turning immediately to your left. Follow the wire fence along, keeping it on your left-hand side. Leave the field by the kissing gate and walk across the narrow wooden bridge over the shallow and cool river and out into the field beyond. Cross this field and walk into the next one ahead of you.

In this second field, keep a sharp lookout when you cross it. Somewhere in this general area to the right of the footpath (3) are the remains of a Roman Villa, and the footpath passes close by it.

The excavations undertaken in 1876 and 1961 uncovered the site of a Roman Villa with mosaics, a Tesselated pavement and Painted wall plaster. This villa began as a small rectangular block of rooms and was later developed into a winged corridor house. For further details, see the website which is located at www.ancientmonuments.info/end0786-roman-villa-900yds-820m-nw-of-parish-church.

Walk across this field and along the well-marked path. Head towards the church tower in the distance. As you breast the rise of the furthest field you will find a beautiful wooden bench that has been placed there for the benefit of the local population. Pause here to look back on at the scenery that now lies unfolded before you.

Keep the church of St Mary Magdalene on your left as you enter the small Dorset village of Thornford. During April and May, the churchyard is ablaze with yellow Cowslips. Pass beneath the huge tree to the road ahead, turning left (4).

Almost immediately you will need to turn right into Boot Lane, keeping the school on your left. At the end of Boot Lane and at the road junction, turn right (5). Walk on through the village and here you will find The Kings Arms, the local village pub.

In front of it is a clock tower that has been dedicated to mark the 60th Anniversary of Queen Victoria in 1897. The electric lighting that was installed to light up the clock was dedicated to the men of the village who had fought in the Second World War. The pub has some garden and wooden benches with seats in it. Its web site can be found at www.kings-arms-thornford.com and that displays its menus and opening times. (Retrieved from the internet 10th January 2018).

Come out of The King's Arms and turn right (6) into Church Street. Look out for the Coffee Tavern, now a private house, but still bearing its distinctive name. In the wall you should be able to spot a separate brick which dates the house as being built in 1796.

Follow the road on down and just past the Old School House, turn left (4) towards the church once more. Follow the footpath exactly the 2.3 Kilometres back to Bradford Abbas and where you left your car.

Trent, Dorset –
The Archbishop's Walk.

Distance: approximately 2.4 kilometres.
Time: 40 minutes.

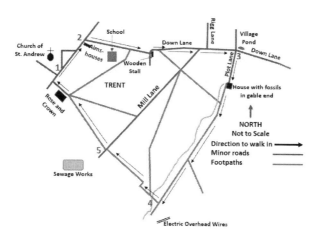

This short and mostly level easy walk will take you through the picturesque and historic village of Trent (population about 301) and invite you to view the last resting place of the 99th Archbishop of Canterbury, Lord Fisher, who died on the 15th September 1972. This was the very same Archbishop who crowned Queen Elizabeth II. History also records that King Charles II of England briefly stayed at the home of a staunch Royalist, Colonel Francis Wyndham, in Trent House, to take a secret respite from the pursuing Roundheads.

Make your way to the village of Trent, Dorset. If you are travelling from Yeovil it can be found about 2½ kilometres north of the main A30 road heading towards Sherborne.

Find somewhere to park near the Church at Grid Reference ST 589 184, Global Positioning System co-ordinates 50° 57' 52.87" North, 2° 35' 09.30" West. For SatNav use DT9 4SL. The walk starts at a height of about 45 metres above sea level and at its lowest is 40 metres. The highest point of the walk is about 56 metres.

Park somewhere near the (1) Church of St. Andrew, and before you enter it you will find a large old stone cross, and in front of this there is a round marker in the ground. This is the memorial to Lord Fisher and his wife, although there

9

is another inside the church. Archbishop Fisher is buried in a crypt. This is also only one of three churches in Dorset that boasts a spire.

Enter the church porch and stop and smile at the sign that says: 'All persons are requested to take off their Pattens and Clogs before entering the church'. Pattens were worn outdoors over a normal shoe up until the early twentieth century and held in place by leather or cloth bands, with a wooden or later wood and metal sole. They were used to elevate the foot above the mud and dirt (including human waste and animal droppings) on the street, in a period when road and urban paving were hardly in existence.

Inside the Church of St. Andrews, the sixteenth century wooden bench ends are ornately carved in various designs ranging from a stag to four birds. In the North Chapel, you will find a wonderful old table and a set of four chairs. You cannot enter this part of the church, but a stone step gives you a grandstand view of the contents. In the South part, you will find the Cope and Mitre (if not loaned out at the time of your visit) that once belonged to the 99th Archbishop of Canterbury, Lord Fisher. What is not so well known is that this Archbishop was also a Free Mason.

Leave the church and proceed left along the road. Opposite the old alms-houses (Turners Close), turn (2) right. A road sign-post informs you that Sherborne is some 4 miles distant; it also points the way towards the village hall. Cross over the road on to the left-hand side and walk through the village on the elevated footpath which can be as high as two feet (about 55 centimetres) above the road.

Go past the school and just after passing "Fisher's Close" on your left, you will find that the spirit of local enterprise is not dead, for a covered wooden stall appears on the far side of the road on the sharp bend. Here local children sell their wares, mostly chicken and duck eggs, to earn their pocket money.

Bear around to the left and stroll on ahead. Along the way you will pass thatched cottages, the Post Office and Stores and the red village phone box. After about 150 metres from the phone box you will need to make a sharp right into Plot Lane.

Before you do, you will find to your front the village (3) pond. Look carefully and you may see a shoal of small Rudd (colourful fish) that inhabit it. The water is fed by a stream and during the winter months is generally very cold, although in very hot weather during the summer and autumn periods it can get Blanket Weed.

Turn into Plot Lane. Follow the tarmac road down to the very end. When you come to the last house that seems to bar your way, go to the right of it and pick up the public foot path. Pause here and look closely at the gable end of this house. Set into it are several large fossils, mostly Ammonites and Clams. Also etched into the wall by the garden gate you can see the inscribed legend that indicates that the house was probably built in 1855.

Walk along the foot path and follow the stream on. Ignore the first wooden bridge on your right and walk on and out into the field beyond. Keep the stream on your right and walk into the next field.

Just before the electric overhead cables, turn right over the stream, crossing by a (4) bridge. Walk straight ahead and uphill towards the church steeple in the distance.

As you come towards the brow of the hill pick up the hedge line and follow it along, keeping it on your left. Start walking downhill, crossing over a tarmac road (5) and over a wooden bridge and up the field. Aim to walk between the thatched house (the Rose and Crown Inn) and the church tower and steeple. This will bring you back to where you parked your car.

The Rose and Crown is a little Dorset village pub, and as such it does not keep town hours. Its website can be viewed at www.theroseandcrowntrent.co.uk/ (retrieved from the internet on 3rd September 2017).

Yeovil, Somerset -
The Three Follies Walk.

Distance: approximately 5.9 kilometres.
Time: 1½ hours.

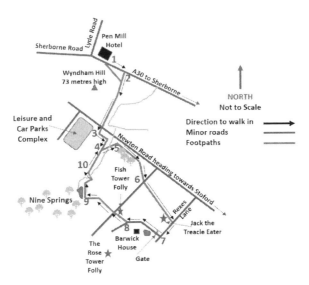

If you contact the Pen Mill Hotel (Telephone 01935 423 081 or visit their website which can be found at www.penmillhotel.co.uk), it is almost certain that the landlord will grant you permission to stop in his ample car park while you undertake this adventure.

The walk involves meandering through a long wood with a gentle incline to the top of the hill above Yeovil. You will also pass close to the Jack the Treacle Eater folly which was built some 230 years ago. From there you will then go through Barwick Park with its beautiful lake and a stunning view across to the Rose Tower Folly. This will lead you up to another folly, the Fish Tower. Finally, you will stand on the crown of the hill above the Nine Springs Country Park, walking along its outskirts before finally returning to your car.

Make your way to Yeovil, Somerset (population about 30,378 in March 2011). The Pen Mill Hotel can be found just off the main A30 road between Yeovil and Sherborne at Grid Reference ST 568 163, Global Positioning System co-ordinates 50° 56' 41.45" North, 2° 36' 56.81" West. For SatNav use BA21 5DB. The walk *starts at a height of about 40 metres above sea level and at its lowest is about 29 metres. The walk reaches, at its highest point, about 83 metres.*

With the Pen Mill Hotel (1) behind you, turn left and walk down the busy A30 towards Sherborne. Cross over the road by means of the Pelican Crossing (2). Follow the path and within a hundred metres of doing so you will find an area surrounded by Buddleia Bushes that, on a warm day, will probably be thronged with many varieties of butterfly including Peacocks, White Admirals, Common Browns, Orange Tips etc. This shrub is often known as The Butterfly Bush.

Arranged in a circular pattern you will see old railway sleepers which depict the link with Pen Mill Station, just over the boundary fence. Walk on along the path for some way, which is also a bicycle track, and pass under the old railway bridge. Turn immediately left (3) here and follow the path around. Just after it bears to the right, cross over the stream by means of the wooden (4) bridge. Follow the path through a newly wooded area. Go through the gateway and head for Newton Copse to your front.

Where the woodland begins, go over the stile (5) and enter it. Follow the path through the wood, with Newton Road lying beneath you and to your left.

Leave the wood and pass over a track and into a field at your front by means of a stile. Walk across the field and leave via the metal gate and down the steps (6) into Two Tower Lane. In front of you is a track called Jack the Treacle Eater Lane.

Cross over the metalled road and go past the large boulder placed in front of the lane to stop cars illegally using it. Carry on down this track for about ¾ of a kilometre. Towards the end of this lane you will find, on your right-hand side, Jack the Treacle Eater's Tower.

Local legend has it that the owner of Barwick Park once had a servant named Jack, who he used to send on a regular basis by coach to London to carry messages for him. Whenever he went he used to take his favourite sandwiches to eat on the journey, which of course were treacle sandwiches.

The statue atop the tower is made of bronze and the figure is of the fabled messenger to the Gods, the winged Hermes.

At the end of this long lane you will come across a tarmac road named locally as Rexe's Hollow Lane. Turn right here and follow it along. Within 200 metres or so turn right into Barwick (7) Park, passing beneath an old Horse Chestnut tree and through the original ham stone gate posts. Walk along the tracks and by the green metal gates (usually locked) pass through the gap purposefully left on the right-hand side for walkers. The public footpath runs along the road that leads to Barwick House. The large pond in front of the house is home to many types of wild fowl, particularly the Moorhen and the Coot. During the Second World War years Barwick

House formed part of a large Prisoner of War camp, housing both Italian and German prisoners as well as a Heavy Anti-Aircraft Battery that protected the Westland's airfield.

Follow the outside tarmac road around and then, on the bend just beyond the house, go through the first kissing gate (8) into the field, heading up towards the large tree that can be seen immediately to your front. Over to your left-hand side you will see another folly, The Rose Tower, and straight ahead of you is another named The Fish Tower. If you turn around at this point you will get a clear view of all of Barwick Park's three follies. Follow the footpath across the field and out through the kissing gate and into Two Tower Lane.

Cross over the tarmac road and into the field beyond by means of another kissing gate, walking straight across it and keeping the hedge immediately on your right. Here you will find yourself on Constitution Hill that looms above Yeovil. It has a good view away to the north of Yeovil. Where the hedge suddenly turns to the right, angle slightly left and walk down the steep re-entrant towards Nine Springs Park beneath you, heading towards a large Horse Chestnut tree. At the very bottom of the hill, (9) turn right and walk along the outskirts of the park, keeping it on your left. Soon and on your left-hand side there will appear the largest lake of Nine Springs with its myriads of wild fowl consisting mostly of Swans and several varieties of wild Ducks. Look carefully for swirls in the water that mark large shoals of Rudd sucking insects off the top of the small lake.

Follow the track along and walk past the children's play area. The track passes a farmyard which will appear on your right-hand side. Follow it around, keeping the stream to your right (10).

As you approach the Tanyard area, the river is covered over before it re-appears again. Soon you will arrive at the built-up area which houses the Leisure and Cap Park complex. Follow the pavement around to your right and it will bring you back to the railway bridge. Re-trace your earlier footsteps to the Pen Mill Hotel.

If you still have some energy left, and as an alternative, you can cross over at the end of the car park and walk up the steep Wyndham Hill (it used to be called Windmill Hill). A copse of trees adorns its summit and is recorded on the Ordnance Survey map to be at a height of 73 metres. Look away to your right to get a splendid view of the county of Dorset. Look down towards the A30 and you will see the Pen Mill Hotel invitingly calling you back for some nice cool refreshments or a meal.

Yeovil Country Park, Somerset –
Fairy Grottos and all that!

Distance: approximately 3.1 kilometres.
Time: 1¼ hours.

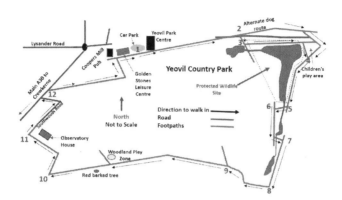

This meander takes you into the local beauty spot known as 'Nine Springs', simply because there are nine springs there that do not go dry, even in the hottest of weather. There are approximately 20 acres of woodland available for you to enjoy in this delightful haven of nature. You will also encounter the magical grotto and, if you are quiet and very lucky, the fairy Majolica herself. Beware! She does not like to be disturbed.

Make your way to Yeovil, Somerset. The Golden Stones Leisure Centre can be found just off the main A30 road between Yeovil and Crewkerne, next to the Coopers Mill Inn and at Grid Reference ST 5553 154, Global Positioning System co-ordinates 50° 56' 11.57" North, 2° 38' 11.29" West. For SatNav use BA20 1QZ.

Make sure that you put enough time on your car parking ticket, which is an All Pay area from 8 a.m. to 6 p.m., Monday to Saturday. When I visited in September 2017 each Sunday was a free parking day.

The walk starts at a height of about 38 metres above sea level and at its lowest is 33 metres. At its highest point, the walk is about 82 metres.

L eave your vehicle in the car park (1) and walk onto the path in front of you. Turn left. The building on your left is the Yeovil Park Centre, and in addition to having information about the park, it has a small café. Walk along the metalled path, ignoring the first track that goes off to your right. You will find shortly that the path splits into three. The first branches left over a bridge, the middle has a wooden gate, and the third goes over another bridge to the right.

Take the middle (3) entrance and pass through the gate. This is a protected wild-life area and dogs are not allowed at all. Keep the stream on your left. (If you are with a dog, go left over the first bridge (2) and at the end of the path bear right around the children's play area to rejoin the walk).

On your right is the bottom and largest pond of Nine Springs, full of fish and wild water life. Amongst the vegetation growing along the stream bank, keep your eyes open for the invasive Himalayan Balsam (*Impatiens glandulifera)*, a large, tall plant with white or pink flowers. During the autumn months their seeds explode open, throwing them for a distance to fall to the ground to grow the following year. Although a pretty plant, if left unchecked they would soon take over any area, so they are regularly weeded to keep them under control.

Keep walking along and you will see a small island, a favourite nesting place for swans and ducks. Follow the path around at this spot and out through the gate (4) to your front. You will now have left the wildlife protected area.

Walk straight ahead for about 20 metres and pass through another gate. Very soon you will come across another Kissing Gate immediately on your right and beneath the towering Beech trees. Pass through it (5) and into the sheltered wood proper. Walk along the well-marked path and cross over the wooden bridge until you meet the concrete path. You need to turn left (6) here and follow the stream, keeping it on your left. Soon you will come across a small waterfall that announces the next pond of Nine Springs.

The area is quite shady and can be quite cool, even in the summer. Look out for the fungi (there are over 20 species reportedly growing here), the Cherry Laurel, Wild Raspberries, Wild Strawberries, Hazelnuts etc.

You will soon be crossing a small wooden and steeply humped bridge. Look carefully to your right and you will see a small tunnel that houses one of the Nine Springs. Walk on ahead and you will find a bigger waterfall on your left, with some steps leading up the hill. Turn left here and cross over the small stream that runs quickly from the third pond and disappears into the waterfall. Turn right (7) under the stone arch and keep the pond on your right. After a little while you will see some steps that lead up to what seems to be an empty place. A little house once stood here. Walk straight ahead and ignore the stone bridge that branches right. Keep the pond on your right.

About 10 metres later, and on your left-hand side, you will find another one of the nine springs that feeds this area of natural beauty. This one rises within the Fairy Grotto. If you are very quiet when you approach this spot you might see the fairy, Majolica, sitting on the flower and brushing her long, flowing hair. It is reputed that while she uses this grotto as her bath-room, the Nine Springs will never run dry.

Follow the stone path ahead, with the stream on your right. Ignore the bridge with the iron railings and keep walking straight ahead.

The stream on your right will soon peter out as the final springs emerge from the hill. The concrete path now finishes and reverts to natural earth. Walk steeply uphill on some (8) steps, following the path around as bears sharply to the right. Ignore the track that goes down to the right and keep going straight ahead.

At the next track junction, bear left (9) (see picture) and from now on ignore all tracks going to the right. Keep to the left-hand track with the field on your left.

As you walk along, and after about 230 metres, you will come across a stand of fir trees. One of them is particularly noticeable, as its bark is almost red. Look to your right and walk down into the Woodland Play Zone. Here you will find the door that leads into the fairy Majolica's home. Well, it is not actually behind this door, for it would not be fair to reveal her true home location, would it.

For the technically minded, the Global Positioning System co-ordinates for this park are at 50° 56' 05.9" North, and 2° 37' 59.8" West. Once you have viewed this, return to your track and the tree with the red bark.

Continue along this track and before long you will get a commanding view of Yeovil's famous airfield lying beneath you and away to the right. After a time, you will come across a stand of mature Oak trees that graces the hedgerow. The track will then start to descend. Go down some steep steps, (10) and follow the track down to the right. Go down some more steps into a re-entrant but ignore the steep steps ahead. Turn right here (11) and head towards the house in front of you, leaving the countryside park.

The very first house on your right is now clad in wood. It used to be a concrete covered bunker that housed the Royal Observer Corps from 1941-1991. In the early 1960's I used to be a part-time member of this group, and most of my Friday evenings were spent below ground there. Recently I have written a book of short stories, The Cider Barn, and is available on Kindle or Amazon. One story follows the adventures of an Observer who was based there during D-Day.

Follow the street (Southwoods Road) to the end, and where it meets the A37 trunk road at Hendford Hill, turn right. After about 10 metres pick up (12) the public footpath on your right and follow it down to the metalled track. Turn sharp let here and then sharp right. The car park where you left your vehicle is in front of you.

Montacute, Somerset –
The Birthday Walk.

Distance: approximately 3.7 kilometres.
Time: 1hour 10 minutes walking.

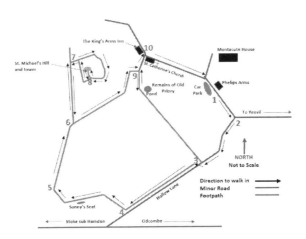

This walk takes in St. Michael's Hill and the village of Montacute with its world renowned Montacute House, a National Trust property. St. Michael's Hill is a Norman Motte and Bailey Castle and this walk will take you to the very top of the hill. This hill is also owned by The National Trust, but entrance to it is free. It is quite a steep walk, and so you will need to have a certain level of personal fitness. It is worth doing, for at its top comes its unique surprise.

I wrote this walk on the day of my 70th birthday, hence the name I have given it. It is also a calorie burner and cardio-vascular work-out.

Drive to the Car Park in the village of Montacute, Somerset (population about 831 in March 2011). It can be found at Grid Reference ST 498 169 and Global Positioning System co-ordinates 50° 56' 58.38" North, 2° 42' 56.99" West.   For SatNav use TA15 6XB. The walk begins at a height of 55 metres and at its lowest point is about 50 metres.   The highest point of the walk, at the tower, is approximately 135.4 metres.

Park your car (1) in the car park and leave it safely locked. Look out for the commemoration plaque on the trough in the car park to George Mitchell

(1826-1901) who championed the National Agricultural Labourers Union. He was born in Montacute.

After having read the plaque, turn to your right, passing The Phelips Arms on your left. You will also pass a T.V., radio and Toy museum that is also well worth a visit (it has its own small and little-known tea-rooms and is very popular for its scrumptious cakes and meals).

Go past the Post Office and immediately turn right (2) into Townsend and follow the road around. Keep walking ahead and the road bends slightly around to the left, keeping Pig Street on your right. Go straight ahead and start walking uphill. As you leave the village, marked by the national road signs, on your right you will observe a footpath sign-posted to Montacute Church. Ignore that one but walk on for about another 5 metres and bear right (3) through the kissing gate and out into the field beyond. Turn left here and walk steadily uphill until you meet the next kissing gate. Go through them and walk ahead.

The aptly named small road called Hollow Lane runs just beneath you and on your left. Keep walking to the top of the field, and at the next footpath gate do not go through it. Turn right (4) here, keeping the far cluster of buildings to your left and follow the path along. Ignore any paths that go down to the right.

Bear left through another footpath gate and soon you will pass beneath some electric wires. Pause for a while on the metal seat that you will come across that bears the legend "Sonny's Seat". Relax and study the beautiful scene which has unfolded before you – the church and the imposing structure of Abbey Farm which all are down in the valley. The tower looms above you and high on the hill. Buzzards often use the updraft from this hill to soar into the sky above, and you may see one if you are lucky.

When you are ready, walk on for another few metres and go through a footpath gate. You will now start walking downhill so follow the track right down to the bottom. In front of you and on the far side of the field there is a wood. Turn right (5) and follow the stone wall along, keeping the wooded are away to the left.

Where the stone wall almost meets the edge of the wood, go through the footpath gate and into the field (6) beyond. Look ahead and walk towards the electric wires to your front, aiming just to the left of the wooded hill beyond. Keep the wood about 50 metres away from you and on your right-hand side. Soon you will come to a wooden gate (7) and stile that takes you into the National Trust property of St. Michael's Hill. Follow the main steep track around all the way up to the top of the hill.

As you walk up the steep hill you will be able to get a tantalising glimpse of the reward that awaits you when you reach its summit. The tower, which was built in 1760, beckons you invitingly towards it. You will be surprised to learn that it has no door on it (September 2017).

This is not the first building to have stood on this site. Originally there would have been a wooden palisade to protect the Bailey. No-one knows when this construction exactly took place, but some believe it to have been built round about 1082 A.D. This building was then lost, and a chapel was erected on this spot in 1102 A.D., where it remained until 1539 A.D. The tower you see before you eventually replaced it.

Walk back down the track, and after about 110 metres, on a sharp bend, the track (8) goes away to the right. Take this track all the way down, ignoring any others that lead off it. Shortly you will come into a flat area that has the appearance of a small field. Turn right here, keeping the tower on your right and above you. This is a flat area, so follow it along until you come to the track you originally walked up on. Turn left and go downhill and out of the wood.

As you pass over the stile, turn left again and retrace your steps downhill, going beneath the power lines until you come to gate that you originally passed (6) through into this field. Turn immediately left here without going through the stile, and, keeping the wall to your right, follow the footpath all the way to the end of the field.

Where the wood and the footpath converge, with a stile prominent on your left and near to the last electric pole in the field, walk on down the hill on the track, keeping the fence and the wood on your left. Soon the path widens out into a dirt track and another gate confronts you. Pass through it and on to a metalled track, keeping Abbey Farm on your right.

It is worth turning right (9) here to walk up the 100 metres or so to view the large pond that appears on your left and in front of what remains on an old Priory. If the conditions are right, you may be able to see the ripple of Carp fins as they angle across the open water and around the Lily pads that occupy it.

Turn around and walk back along the track, heading towards the Church of St. Catherine before you. At the main road (10) junction, with the King's Arms on your left, turn right.

You are now in Middle Street. Walk on for about 200 metres and you will find the entrance to Montacute House on your left and the Car Park where you left your car on the right.

Compton Dundon, Somerset –
The Warrior's Walk

Distance: approximately 4 Kilometres.
Time: 1 hours walking.

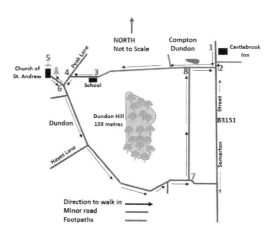

This ramble takes you to the Somerset Levels and takes you up a gentle incline. The village has connections with King Alfred the Great and what is reputed to be the second oldest Yew tree in Britain. I have called it "The Warrior's Walk" in honour of a New Zealand soldier who is buried there.

Drive to the village of Compton Dundon, Somerset (population about 705 in March 2011). It can be found on the B3151 between the towns of Somerton and Street at Grid Reference ST 489 328 and Global Positioning System co-ordinates 51° 05' 30.16" North, 2° 43' 46.64" West. For SatNav use TA11 6PR. The walk begins at a height of about 12 metres above sea level and is also its lowest point. Its highest point is approximately 32.4 metres.

Find somewhere to park up in the centre (1) of the village. Walk back towards Somerton along the B3151, passing the local pub, the Castlebrook Inn, on the left-hand side. Move across to the right-hand side of the road and go through the national speed limit signs. After about 8 metres (2) you will find a kissing gate on the right that leads you into a field.

Pause for a while to view the impressive Dundon Hill, a nature reserve to your immediate front, that soars 103 metres above sea level. In ancient times there used to be a beacon on the hill and it was known as Dundon Beacon. It is strange to think that in King Alfred's time this land upon which you are now standing was still marshland and Dundon Hill, an ancient Iron Age hill fort, stood alone as an island in the middle of the marshes.

Follow the footpath through five fields, keeping the hill on your left. On your right-hand side and as you walk through the first field you should be able to glimpse a manmade pond through the sparse hedge, complete with a little rowing boat.

In the last field, there are some paving slabs laid on the ground. Be careful if it is wet as the slabs can be quite slippery. This path then leads you into a lane with the village school on your (3) left. Ahead of you the tower of the fourteenth century church of St Andrews looms above you, dominating the landscape. In front of it you can view the Yew tree you will soon be visiting.

The lane now joins another lane, aptly called Peak Lane. Turn left here (4) and then very shortly afterwards turn right and walk up to the (5) Church of St. Andrew's. On entering the churchyard, the first thing that impresses you is the old and gnarled Yew tree that dominates the area (see picture on the book cover). It has been certified as being 1700 years of age, or to put it into perspective, it was an old tree before the legendary King Alfred the Great frequented the area. This certificate can be found inside the church on the south wall towards the bell tower end of the church. But this is not why we are here.

Walk down over the churchyard and into the graveyard extension. Here you will

find a magnificent marble headstone dedicated to Trooper William Dawbin, of the New Zealand Wellington Mounted Rifles. During the Gallipoli campaign of 1915 he was severely wounded in the spine and brought back by hospital ship to the military hospital at Netley, Hampshire, where he was tended. Sadly, he succumbed to his wounds.

Normally soldiers would be buried where they died, but his father, also named William (who was living in New Zealand at the time), had been born and raised in Dundon village before he had emigrated. He had his son's body brought to his home village and interred there. Local legend has it that his father's house overlooked the churchyard where William's body now lies.

The white marble headstone has a fully saddled and riderless horse sculptured at the top of it, with a rifle and fixed bayonet dominating the left-hand side of the headstone. The right-hand side has a carving of a Trooper's pick and shovel. At the base of the headstone you will find a sculptured hat and stirrups. Not surprisingly the whole beautiful marble headstone weighs in at a ton and looks as though it has just been placed there.

As you go about this wonderful country of ours you will also see a lot of statues dedicated to long gone soldiers sitting on a horse. An interesting fact about these statues is this: if the horse has one front leg raised off the ground it meant that the rider died from wounds received; two front legs raised meant that the rider died in battle; if the horse's two front legs are firmly on the ground it meant that the rider had not died in or because of a battle but had died normally. Alas, this is just popular fiction. The truth is that the artist sculpted what he thought was the best shape for the statute, and they usually gave no thought as to how that soldier had died.

Leave the churchyard and go back down into Peak Lane, turning (6) right. Follow the road along and walk through the village. There is a stone bench, dated 2000, on the right-hand side of the road for any weary traveller to sit and rest for a while.

Walk on out of the village, keeping the hill on your left. You will then start to go slightly downhill. You will soon come across some iron railings that mark the boundary of a field. Keep these on your right and walk down to where the road bends sharply to the right. There is a public footpath sign in front of you pointing the way to your left. Go through the metal gate (7) and pass out into the field beyond.

Follow this footpath along for five fields, keeping the hill on your left. Away to the distance and off to the right you will see a large tower on the horizon, rising through the woodland. This is the monument erected to the memory of Admiral Sir Samuel Hood and is a Grade II listed building.

Soon you rejoin the footpath (8) that you walked along earlier. Turn right here and across the final field to the B3151. Turn left and walk back towards your car.

The Castlebrook Inn itself is well worth a visit. The pub serves excellent food and has a huge car park. It also sells an extensive range of real ales and, most importantly, some proper Somerset scrumpy! Its website can be found at www.castlebrookinn.com (retrieved from the internet 8th January 2018) and the telephone number is 01458 448902. For SatNav use TA11 6PR.

East Coker, Somerset -
The Poet's Walk.

Distance: approximately 3.4 Kilometres.
Time: 1½ hours.

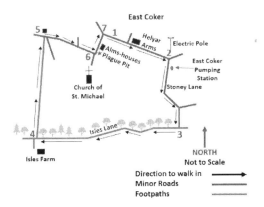

The world-renowned poet and writer, Thomas Stearns Eliot (T.S. Eliot) was born on the 26th September 1888 in St. Louis, Missouri, of an old New England family. He died on the 4th January 1965 in Kensington, London. In 1939, he wrote 'Old Possum's Book of Practical Cats' which went on to be turned into the smash hit musical, "Cats."

A naturalised Briton, he passed away in London and expressed the wish that his ashes be interred in the church of St. Michael's in East Coker. His ancestor, Andrew Eliot, left this village to travel to America in the seventeenth century.

The village of East Coker (population about 1,667 in March 2011) can be located at Grid Reference ST 540 123 and Global Positioning System co-ordinates 50° 54' 30.65" North, 2° 39' 16.24" West. For SatNav use BA22 9JR.

The village is about 2 miles from the town of Yeovil, which is north of the village. Little lanes and thatched houses are a common feature of the place and a small stream trickles silently through it. The walk is circular and is mostly along bridleways and should take no more than an hour and a half to complete, even at an easy pace. Along the way you encounter some gentle inclines and a few stiles. Each stile is made so that a dog can pass through it.

The starting point is also the walk's lowest point at about 55 metres above sea level. At its highest point it is about 115 metres.

The local inn is The Helyar Arms. Be warned, this is a popular food venue and one of the 'In' places of Somerset to dine at. Consequently, the car park is generally full. Please do not park there without the permission of the owner.

The inn can be contacted on 01935 862332 and its web site can be found at www.helyararms.com (retrieved from the internet 16th September 2017). Accommodation is available here if required.

Drive to East Coker, Somerset (1) and find somewhere to park safely. Walk along the road in a generally easterly direction, keeping 'Silverweed Cottage' on your left. After about 350 metres you will encounter the road sign that informs you that you are at "Coker Marsh". A large electric pole with a transformer is there on your left and confirms your position. Turn right (2) and walk into Stoney Lane, going past the enclosed and labelled East Coker Pumping Station on the left. Walk along and walk gently uphill on the tarmac lane, following it around a noticeably sharp left-hand bend and then another very sharp right-hand bend. The tarmac of the road now begins to break up and revert to its former state of a track way. Follow this track up to a 'T' junction (3) and turn right. The direction has a footpath sign-post that bears the legend "Isles Lane Moors Plantation – 1 mile."

Walk along the wide track, fringed on your right by massive old beech trees. During the spring month's the banks of the hedges are covered with wild flowers of every description, including wonderful arrays of wood anemone's, primroses, bluebells, white and blue violets etc., to name but a few.

After walking about a kilometre along this track you will espy Isles Farm down the slight hill and on your left. Directly opposite the farm lane you need to turn right (4), walking up the steps and into the woodland. A footpath signpost bearing the legend "Coker Court Park – ½ mile" points the way. Walk directly through the woodland in a north-easterly direction, heading uphill and crossing a track as you do so.

Pass over a stile and into the green parkland beyond. Massive tree stumps still lie where they have fallen.   Walk straight ahead, aiming to walk slightly left of a large clump of Oak trees that can be seen to your front and over the crest of the small hill. After you reach the crest of this relatively slight hill you start to descend, keeping this clump of trees to your right. Walk directly towards a cottage that can be seen in front of you and in the near distance. Pass over another stile, by a metal gate, and make your way down to the cottage. Go over another stile and into the unpaved track in front of the cottage.

Walk ahead a few metres to the large bend in the road (5), making sure that you keep to the left-hand part of the lane and walk downhill. Go straight ahead on this track until you come to the 'T' junction where you will find the old alms houses immediately in front of you (6).

Turn right here and take the footpath up towards the church, pausing at the end of the row of alms houses to look at a burial site. There is a memorial headstone placed here to commemorate the 70 inhabitants of East Coker who died from the plague when that terrible disease wrought havoc in the village during the year 1645 A.D.

As you walk into the churchyard take time to look at the gravestone that is the second headstone back immediately as you enter. It marks the spot where Police Constable Nathaniel Cox lies, brutally killed by three men who beat him to death in 1876. Those three men were found guilty of manslaughter and sentenced to 24 years transportation each.

Enter the church of St Michael's itself through the porch way. Be aware that as you enter the church there is a sudden step up from the porch, so look out for it. The church is very ancient, and the slabs of stone are also uneven. Immediately to your right you will see the plaque that marks T.S. Eliot's final resting place. A commemorative plaque to the poet, T.S. Eliot, and on the eastern wall of the Church, bears his epitaph. These were lines chosen from one of his poems of the Four Quartets: "In my beginning is my end. In my end is my beginning." His second poem of the Four Quartets is called 'East Coker' and was published in 1940.

On the south wall, there is a beautiful brass plaque that records the history of another well-known East Coker man, (although he is not buried here), Sir William Dampier. He was born on the 5th September 1651 at Hymerford House in East Coker and died on the 8th March 1715 in London. He was a well-known English buccaneer, sea captain, author and scientific observer of the time and was the first Englishman to explore and map parts of New Holland, Australia and New Guinea. He was also the first person to circumnavigate the world three times.

Leave the church and go back to the almshouses, walking down and passing the small grass park on your right. At the road junction (7) turn right and return to your car.

Hatch Beauchamp, Somerset -
The Hero of Rorke's Drift Walk.

Distance: approximately 8.7 Kilometres.
Time: 2½ hours.

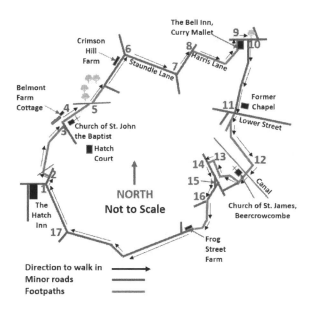

The Church of St. John the Baptist lies on the village outskirts and in the grounds of a large house, Hatch Court. Buried next to the Church is one of the heroes from the 1879 Zulu War in Africa at Rorke's Drift, John Rouse Merriott Chard, who died from a terrible disease.

Another little-known hero also rests here, the man who, during World War One, helped to create the famous Canadian regiment, Princess Patricia's. At one time he was also the Member of Parliament for Taunton.

Hatch Beauchamp is a small village (population about 620) that lies about 5 miles south east of the county town of Taunton. It can be found just off the A358 and approximately midway between Ilminster and Taunton.

The beautiful village is located at Map Reference ST 302 205 and its Global Positioning System coordinates are 50° 58'48.75" North and 2° 59'41.98" West. For SatNav, use Post Code TA3 6SG.

The walk is circular and passes over pastureland and along several minor roads. It starts at an elevation of 58 metres above sea level and at its lowest point it is 29 metres. At its highest point the walk reaches 87.6 metres.

In the centre of the village and by the bus stop lies The Hatch Inn, an old 18th century coaching house. Turn right here into Station Road and find somewhere to park your car. As always, if you would like to park in the inn's Car Park please check with the owner first. The telephone number of the inn is 01823 480245. It can also be contacted through their website at www.thehatchinn.co.uk (retrieved from the internet on the 17th September 2017). The pub is locally sourced for its food and has accommodation available.

Having parked your car in Station Road (1), walk back to the signpost opposite the Hatch Inn which directs you towards the Parish Church. You will notice that the sign says that this small road is also a part of the National Cycle Route Number 33. Walk along this small road for about 50 metres. On your right there is an ancient wall with a blocked old arched doorway and made of the local blue stone. Take the sign-posted footpath on the left (2), passing through the gate and through the well-kept wood, and going over a metalled lane.

Follow the footpath sign and keep the wooden railings of the field on your left. On your right you should see the interesting circular building that forms part of Hatch Court, a building noted as one of the most beautiful houses in the south west and is one of the most outstanding examples of Palladian architecture in the whole country. It was built of Bath stone in 1750 by Thomas Prowse, of Axbridge. Hatch Court can be glimpsed across the park and away to your right.

Soon you will come to a concrete driveway with some wooden gates on your left and the church immediately to your front. You will need to come back to these gates shortly, but in the meanwhile go across the driveway, and if it is open, into the St. John the Baptist Church (3).

Inside the church is the first surprise. Often missed by visitors because the plaque is on the floor and just inside the church entrance, is the memorial to Brigadier A. Hamilton Gault, D.S.O., E.D., C.D., who once lived in Hatch Court and lies buried here.

He was the co-founder of the famous Princess Patricia's Canadian Light Infantry Regiment, the last privately raised regiment of the British Army (he had donated $100,000 to help equip it), and with whom he fought in France during World War One, winning great honour and glory for the regiment. He first served as a Major as the second-in-command, and finally commanded it during the Second Battle of Ypres. Gault was wounded and had to relinquish his command. He was finally given complete command of Princess Patricia's in November 1918 *(despite having lost a leg at Sanctuary Wood at the Battle of Mount Sorrell in 1916) and remained with them until their demobilization.*

Inside the small church you will also find a stained-glass window in the chancel erected in the memory of Colonel John Chard. This is best viewed from the inside with the light shining through it.

John Rouse Merriott Chard V.C. was born in Plymouth, Devon, on the 21st December 1847. He had been nominated as the new Commanding Officer of a unit in Perth, Scotland but was unfortunately not able to take up the appointment. He had cancer of the tongue and died from this terrible disease on the 1st November 1897, still a serving officer, and living with his brother in the Rectory at Hatch Beauchamp (his brother was the Rector of St John's Church at the time).

As a 32 years old Royal Engineers officer, Lieutenant Chard was building a bridge in Natal when he was placed in command of the British Defences at the Supply Station at Rorke's Drift. In 1964 a film was made starring Stanley Baker as Lieutenant Chard and Michael Caine as Lieutenant Bromhead.

On the morning of the 22nd January 1879, the Zulu army massacred a large British force at Isandlwana, South Africa. Later that afternoon another army of about 4,000 Zulu warriors, who had not taken place in the original battle at Isandlwana, attacked the Commissariat Store and hospital at Rorke's Drift. The place was manned by a detachment of 139 men, mostly of the 2nd Battalion, 24th Regiment of Foot (but other regiments were also there, of which 35 were receiving treatment in the hospital at the time). Despite fierce attacks all that afternoon and night, Lieutenant Chard and his men held out.

The next morning the Zulus withdrew, leaving their many dead behind them. For this battle Lieutenant Chard and 10 other men, including the other officer involved, Lieutenant Bromhead, were awarded the Victoria Cross. This remains today as the most Victoria Crosses ever awarded for a single engagement.

Leave the church and walk around to its south side, and next to it you will find the pinkish coloured granite cross that marks the final resting place of this hero. It is a well visited spot and you will see much evidence of this in the form of poppies and poppy crosses. When I visited a poem, dedicated to the Royal Engineers, had been placed upon his grave.

Leave the churchyard and return to the wooden gates on your right and pass through them. Keep the beautiful pond (private) and Belmont Farm Cottage (4) on your left as you walk straight ahead, keeping the churchyard to the right. When you come to the concrete road, turn right for about 50 metres. Here the footpath marker indicates where the path leaves the road and angles away to the right, across the field (5) and towards a high tree. Follow it.

At the woods edge, walk out on to the tarmac road and turn left. Go along the road for some way, passing Crimson Hill Farm. Shortly afterwards, there is a house on your left-hand side. At the road junction (6) turn right into Staundle Lane and follow the direction-posted road towards Curry Mallet. At the next road junction, turn left and follow the sign-post that directs you towards the village of Curry Mallet (7).

Walk past a sign that says "Doble Close", and after about 20 metres turn right (8) down a wide dirt track (Harris Lane), keeping a red brick house (Lyddon's Farm) to your left. Follow the track on down into the village, turning left and up another track just before a tarmac road. Keep the wall on your right and walk the 50 metres or so along it. The Bell Inn, Curry Mallet, is immediately on your right (9).

This pub's address is Higher Street, Curry Mallet, Taunton, Somerset TA3 6SY. More information about it is held on www.thebellinncm.com (retrieved from the web 17th September 2017). It is a typical village pub with wooden beams. Open planned, it has a large wood burning stove situated in its centre. It has been described by locals as "not quite in the middle of nowhere but on the outskirts of somewhere."

Leave the pub, if you have visited it, and walk along the road for a short way, turning almost immediately right by (10) the Horse Chestnut tree (sign-posted Beer Crowcombe) and walk along the tarmac road, passing the huge font situated in a sort of courtyard of a house on your left and go around the sharp bend.

Walk on for a while until you come to Pope's Cross. There will be a converted chapel on your left-hand side. Walk straight over the road and on to the dirt track to your front (11) keeping 'April Cottage' on your right. Go some way down the track until you come to a metal kissing gate on your left that opens out on to a field. Go through it.

You now need to angle left across this field to another gate, passing through it and out into the next field. At this point you will need to again angle left across this field, clipping the edge of a small pheasant copse away to your front and on your left. Keep the hedge on your left.

Walk ahead and through a metal gate and out into another field. Away to your right you will see the church tower of St. James' in Beercrowcombe.   Keep this hedge on your right and walk on up and along the field.

At the end of the field, turn right and through a pedestrian gate. Just a little way up you will see another gate flanked by the memory of the Second World War, a set of 'Dragon's Teeth' anti-tank (12) concrete blocks immediately above what remains of the old Chard to Bridgwater Canal.

This water-way was some 13½ miles in length and started at the Bridgwater and Taunton canal.   It ran from Creech St. Michael and during its journey it went over four aqueducts, through three tunnels and four inclined planes to Chard.   It was completed in 1842 but never was commercially viable and finally closed to traffic in 1868.   The old branch railway line (now closed), ran from Chard to Taunton, and for most of its journey followed the line of the old canal. The railway opened on the 8th May 1863, five years before the canal was finally closed.

This canal formed a part of the World War Two defences and was part of the Somerset Stop Line. Cross the canal, which still contains water, by means of the little wooden bridge, and walk up its bank, heading towards the church to your front.

Pass through the wooden gate and into the churchyard itself, walking to the far end of the churchyard and out of it by means of the other small wooden pedestrian gate. Turn immediately left and follow the wooden fence along.

Go through another gate and out into the field beyond, keeping the hedgerow to your left. Walk around until you come to another gate which leads you into a (13) narrow pathway. Follow it around and another gate opens into what looks like a private garden, which it is. The footpath goes through here to the road, and if you look ahead you will see the footpath sign pointing towards you from the road.

On joining this road turn left (14) and walk into the village. When you reach the 'T' junction with is direction indicator pointing towards Stewley, turn right (15) at the grassy triangle. Walk on down the hill until you come across a "Road liable to flooding" sign. Just after this sign, pass over the concrete agricultural bridge (16) and through the metal gate into a field. A footpath sign directs you across it and in the far corner of the field to your right you will see another gate. Go through this gate and out into the field beyond.

Walk up the hill keeping to the right and as you start going downhill make for the far right-hand corner of the field. Exit the field to enter a little farm lane and turn right. Follow it along and shortly you will find Frog Street Farm on your right. Go on to the metalled road and ignore where the road bends to the right (sign-posted Beer Crowcombe). Walk straight ahead (sign-posted Hatch Beauchamp).

Follow the road, passing over an old railway bridge which crosses the now defunct Chard Junction to Taunton Town branch railway, a victim of the savage Dr. Beeching railway cuts.

Walk along the road and follow the road sign that points you towards "Hatch Beauchamp ¾". Go under the electric wires and keep the cottage on the right. Just after you pass through the 30-m.p.h. national speed limit signs you will come to a 'T' junction. Turn right (17) and follow the sign-post that says, "Hatch Beauchamp ½". Follow the road back to where you left your car.

Corton Denham, Somerset –
The Flying Submariner.

Distance: approximately 5.8 kilometres.
Time: 2 hours walking.

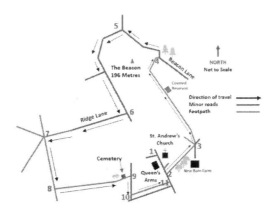

Although the village has a Post Code that causes most people to think that the village is in the County of Dorset, it is not. It is a definite Somerset village as any of the locals in the Queens Arms would be quick to point out. Surrounded by steep hills and rolling countryside, the area also has some outstanding views.

Buried in the small cemetery in the village lies a holder of the nation's highest honour for valour, the Victoria Cross. More about the World War Two raid on the Tirpitz later.

Corton Denham is a small village with a population of about 210 souls. It snuggles below a high and protecting ridge and is located at Grid Reference ST 635 225, Global Positioning System coordinates 51° 00' 01.86" North, 2° 31' 16.29" West. It is about 7 miles north east of Yeovil.   For SatNav, use Post Code DT9 4LR to put you close to the Church.

The walk is circular but does have a stiff hill to climb.   It starts at a height of about 100 metres above sea level, and at its lowest point is about 86.8 metres. It then rises to 194 metres.

F ind somewhere to park close to the Church of St. Andrew's. On the main road through the village (1) walk past the Post Office letter box and the old-fashioned stone drinking trough with a stone bench donated by the local Woman's Institute on your left. The cobbled path between them leads directly up to the church should you wish to view it.

Walk ahead, keeping Middle Ridge Lane on your right. Go past the Queen's Arms and the man-made track turning up the hill. After about 70 metres there is a gate on your left (2) with a footpath sign. Go through the gate, and angle left across the field, keep the electric poles to the right. Aim for the gap between the trees at the top of the grassland ahead of you, going steadily uphill all the time.

When you get to this point with the church on your left, look up to the top of the ridge and you will see an electric pole at the summit and slightly to your left. Walk on upwards towards this post and up the towering Corton Hill. You will be ascending about 80 metres from this point at a steady rising rate.

Keep walking uphill. Just before you get to the crest you will pass through another small gate. Make sure that you have the electric lines on your right. Carry on up the hill and you will come to another metal gate in front of you that leads into a little lane. There are two paths on your left. Take the top path (3) that leads upwards towards a stone wall.

This part of the walk is not so steep now and you will get wonderful views across the valley. The church in Corton Denham majestically imposes its presence upon you. Once you get to the crest of the hill, walk along it, keeping the wall on your right.

If you look across three fields to your right, you will note a curious sight. A white building, which was once the control tower for a World War Two airfield, HMS Heron II, still stands there. Today it is a private dwelling (Sigwells House) and it is lived in.

As you pass through the gate you will see a covered reservoir on your right. The stone wall now gives way to a fence. Follow this fence along to the end, about 100 metres before the very peak of Corton Hill and it will lead you around to the right and through another gate. Head towards some Scots Pine trees that are facing you.

On the top of the hill lies a Trig Point with the height noted as 196 metres above sea level. This is known as The Beacon. There is no public footpath to it.

The fence then turns right. Follow this fence towards the metal gate and pass (4) through it and out into Beacon Lane. Turn left and start walking downhill.

As you descend you will see the tall hill immediately to your front that is called Parrock Hill. If you glance away to your right you will see the large and flat-topped Cadbury Castle, a hill that it is said was once called Camelot and supposedly the home to the legendary King Arthur. A bronze age shield was once excavated there. We do know that it was a Bronze and Iron Age hill fort and once occupied by the Durotriges and Dobunni tribes who fiercely resisted the Roman occupation.

At the road junction and with Parrock Hill immediately to your front, turn left (5). Keep your eyes and ears open for cyclists as this section of the walk is also part of Route 26 of the National Cycle network. As you round a bend the church of the village comes into view in the distance. Walk on and down into the village of Corton Denham.

Turn right into Ridge Lane (6). It is initially a tarmac lane that eventually gives out to a bridleway. This lane starts at about 100 metres above sea level, and the gentle incline will take you up to about 136 metres. On the way, you will pass the Corton Ridge covered reservoir on your right-hand side.

As you start to go down-hill you are confronted with two metal gates to your front. Take the left-hand gate and pass through it (7). Walk along the field, keeping the high bank and hedge on your left. Look down the valley below you to see a large set of farm buildings. When you get almost opposite these buildings, look out for the gap in the hedge with steps that takes you up and through a gate (8). Walk straight ahead for three fields, heading slightly to the right of the church tower. The path is well-marked, so you should have no problem following it.

Once you are across the last field you will enter a small dirt lane. Walk on downhill with the cemetery on your left side for about 80 metres. Enter the cemetery through the gates. At the top end of the centre of the cemetery you will find a gravestone of a true World War Two hero.

Basil Charles Godfrey Place (as indicated by his headstone, he preferred to be known as Godfrey) was born on the 19th July 1921 and died on the 27th December 1994, aged 73, and is buried in Corton Denham Cemetery, Somerset. He won his Victoria Cross during World War Two for his part in an attack by British midget submarines on the German battleship Tirpitz. Godfrey Place was one of the few submariners that have successfully transferred to the Fleet Air Arm. During the Korean War, he saw active service flying in a Sea Fury of Number 801 Naval Air Squadron.

Leave the cemetery behind you and walk on down the lane where very shortly you will encounter a tarred road. Turn right here (9) and follow it along for about 300 metres. Where the road bends sharply around to the right there is a metal pedestrian gate on your left. Go through this gate (10) and out into the little fenced area you cross to get to another stile. Pass over it and walk a little way to the next stile, passing over a small stream just beyond it. Walk straight ahead across the field, aiming for the clump of trees immediately to your front and the prominent metal gate. Go over the stile next to the gate and turn left (11), walking up the tarmac road and through the cutting. After 300 metres you will arrive at The Queen's Arms.

The pub does a good selection of home-made food and pickles, as well as snacks. It also has an excellent variety of local ales and ciders. For the children, there is always some home-made cake or fudge on offer, and even local free-range eggs are available from the pub's own chickens. It can be contacted on 01963 220317 and its web site can be found at www.thequeensarms.com (retrieved from the Internet Tuesday 19th September 2017). From here, walk straight ahead to where you started your walk.

Charleton Horethorne, Somerset –
The Hero of British Somaliland Walk.

Distance: approximately 6.3 kilometres.
Time: 1½ hours.

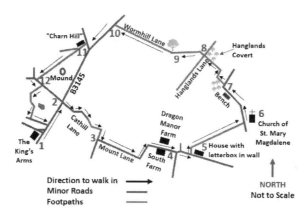

The small village of Charlton Horethorne (population 1,550 in 1994) straddles the busy B3145 Sherborne to Wincanton road about 5 miles north east of Sherborne. The starting point for the walk is the triangle of the village and next to the highly recommended King's Arms. The map reference is ST 664 232 and the Global Positioning Systems co-ordinates are 51° 00' 26.85" North, 2° 28' 44.63" West. Use Post Code DT9 4NL to find the area.

The walk is circular and passes over pastureland and meanders along some countryside roads. The walk starts at a height of about 114.8 metres above sea level and at its lowest about 92 metres. It rises gently to its highest point of about 169 metres. Along the way we will come across the final resting place of another Victoria Cross holder.

Drive into the village and find somewhere to park in the triangle close to a superb pub named the Kings Arms. It really is a hidden gem of Somerset. Its food is highly recommended, and the ales and ciders are a delight to sample.

The traditional fittings also boast a small bar with a sofa and several arm chairs. Its walls are bedecked with paintings and bronze resin statuettes by local artists, and they are for sale. The pub has its own large car park for its customers, and, as usual, should you wish to use it please obtain the landlords permission first. The pub's website can be found at www.thekingsarms.co.uk (retrieved from the internet on the

8th January 2018) and its telephone number is 01963 220281. Across the road from the pub there is a massive bronze map of the village, that is also a wonderful work of art. It is certainly worth viewing.

Next to the pub comes another pleasant surprise, "The Village Shop". There you will be able to find a wide range of local products plus your everyday groceries. There is a fresh food counter that stocks a surprising variety of good quality cheeses, plus hand-made produce including quiches, scotch eggs, pies, deserts and more. They also provide take-away cups of fresh ground coffee and have seating should you wish to consume it there.

Having successfully parked (1) move across the road and proceed in a generally north easterly direction along the B3145, keeping the bronze map of the village and the village green on your left. Go past the wooden Village Hall on your right. About 100 metres later you will encounter a signpost (2) that directs you into Cathill Lane. Follow it and walk up a little gradient with a pretty stream and waterfall on your left. Keep walking along the track and you will soon pass a bungalow called 'Meadow Place' on your right. Initially the little road is tarmac, but this is soon lost and peters out into a long dirt track. Walk along the lane and where the track bends sharply away to the right, follow it down to the road.

Turn left at (3) the road junction and follow the high-hedged country lane along. For part of the way you will have a babbling village brook keeping your company on your right-hand side. Just after the curiously named Dragon Manor Farm you will arrive at a road junction (4). Turn immediately left here and look for the road signpost to Horsington and follow the direction. After about 50 metres you will come across a house with a red post box set in the wall (5). Just before it, turn left through the metal gate and walk along the footpath. It is sign-posted 'St. Mary Magdalene.'

At the end of the little track, pass out into the field immediately to your front and through another metal kissing gate. You will see a row of electric poles crossing the field to your right. Walk towards the church tower ahead of you and some two fields away, keeping the hedge on your left and the electric line on your right. Pass out thought the gate to a small field. Angle left across the field, keeping the pond to your right. Cross over the road and enter the churchyard of St Mary Magdalene (6).

As you enter the churchyard, and just to your left, you will notice a dark coloured slate headstone. Here lies Lieutenant Colonel Eric Charles Twelves Wilson, V.C. As a captain in the East Surrey Regiment he was seconded to the Somaliland Camel Corps in 1939. British Somaliland was invaded by some 350,000 Italian troops it was defended by approximately 1,500 British soldiers. From the 11th through to the 15th August 1940, Captain Wilson occupied an exposed observation post at the Tug Argan Pass, manning a machine gun despite suffering multiple wounds, and being ill with malaria. His position eventually fell after four days of resistance and he was taken as a prisoner-of-war at Adi Ugri in Eritrea. He was wrongly assumed to have been killed in action and was awarded the Victoria Cross, posthumously, in October 1940. His freedom came when the British liberated Eritrea and he was returned to duty in North Africa with the Long-Range Desert Group.

Leave the churchyard and turn right, ignoring the gravel drive to The Old Farmhouse. Walk straight ahead and continue up Stowell Hill and towards the woodland that lies to your front. About 100 metres from the wood you will find a substantial wooden seat placed there during the Millennium year. It is worth stopping just to look at the view behind you and back towards the church.

Walk on up the hill and go around the sharp corner, ignoring the track that runs to the left of the wood. After about 50 metres (7) you will see a footpath sign that directs you up the steep bank with some helpful steps positioned there to aid you. Pass through a little bit of scrubland with a building's ruins on your right. Go over a stile and out into the field over a railway sleeper bridge.

Keep the woodland immediately on your left, heading towards the hedge in the distance. When you reach it, turn right and follow it along. After about 100 metres, and just before the hedge turns a sharp left, you will come across a metal gate. Go through it and out into the field beyond, keeping the hedge on your right.

Walk on down over the fields and head towards the woodland in front of you (Hanglands Covert) and keep the hedge and wood to your right. Pass over a stile into Hanglands Lane but walk straight across it and out over another stile into the field beyond. You are now on the part of the walk that is known as the (8) 'Monarchs Way.'

Angle slightly left towards the top of the hill, passing through two sets of gates and out into another small field directly in front of you. Keep the pond to your front and on your left-hand side as you walk down across the small field and pass over a stile and into another field.

Go through another wooden kissing gate and keep walking downhill, keeping the large metal cow's troughs to either side of you in the fence and hedge boundaries. The village of Charlton Horethorne lies beneath.

Walk downhill towards the metal gate (9) that has a large oak tree slightly to the right of it. When you reach the gate, turn right and follow the dirt track (named Wormhill Lane) along to its conclusion. You now come to a bungalow to your front with a farm on the left (10). Turn left on the little lane and walk on down to rejoin the B3145. Turn immediately right and cross over the busy road to a stile that lies just before (11) "Charn Hill" cottage. Go over it and into the field. With "Charn Hill" cottage behind you, and the road on your left, walk up the small but steep bank ahead of you, and then angle to the right of the top of the mound on Charn Hill. Walk up the hill, keeping the well-defined banks of the Mound on your left, and then at the crest of the hill, start descending towards the right-hand corner of the field. Go over the stile and out into the aptly name Water Lane. Turn left here and follow the road for about 75 metres.

Turn right (12) onto a sign-posted footpath and follow it around to the Charlton Horethorne Millennium Green. There is a deep pond in this area, full of beautiful water lilies and a shoal of darting ornamental fish. Local rules state that children under 8 years of age must be accompanied in this part of the walk. Some while ago, the local school children each had a brick with their name on it built into the wall that stands just behind the pond.

Keeping the shelter on your right, follow the path around and out through a gate into a private road. Turn left and follow the footpath the short distance back out into the Triangle.

Mells, Somerset -
The Soldier Poet and the Politician's Walk.

Distance: approximately 6.4 kilometres
Time: 1½ hours

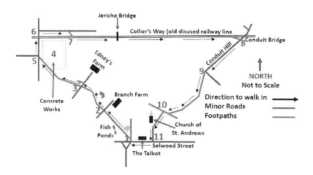

The village of Mells (population 638 in March 2011) is located about 4 miles north-west of Frome and about 10 miles north east of Shepton Mallet. It is almost due north of the A361. The starting point for the walk is set on the road outside The Talbot, the local hostelry in Mells. The map reference is ST 727 492 and the Global Positioning System co-ordinates are 51° 14' 28.71" North, 2° 23' 30.58" West. The SatNav Post Code to use is BA11 3PN.

The walk is circular and at one point follows an old railway line which is now a national cycle route. As such it is paved and extremely easy walking. It takes in some wonderfully unexpected events. At its starting point the walk is about 100 metres above sea level and at its lowest the walk is 97 metres. It rises in some parts to its highest point of about 136 metres, although most of it is over a gentle incline.

Find somewhere to park near the Grade II listed pub. This is an old 17th century coaching house and is also a Free House, although early records indicate that it has stood here since the 14th century. It can be found about 100 metres from the church and is located on the edge of the beautiful Mendip Hills and within the tiny parish of Mells and Vobster. There is plenty of parking on the road near the pub, but should you wish to pre-book a meal then their website is located at www.talbotinn.com (retrieved from the internet on the 8th January 2018) and their telephone number is 01373 812254. It has a good-sized restaurant and well used beer garden.

Walk along Selwood Street in a generally westerly direction which quickly takes you out of the village. At the road junction that comes in from your left, turn right (1) before the bus shelter. This comes just after the gates of Mells Manor with a statue of a dog sitting atop each gate-post carrying out their sentinel duties. Pass through a low stone wall next to the gates and through a pedestrian gate and out into the field.

There are two stiles that leave this field, one to your left and one straight ahead of you. You need to take the left footpath and angle left across the field, keeping a small clump of trees to your right and Mells Manor at your back. Walk across to the small stile next to the gate and pass through it. Walk down towards the left-hand hedge at a point just after the fish ponds. Cross over the stream into the field by means of the stone bridge that spans the bridge.

Here you need to angle right across this field to the top right-hand corner. The hedge to your left disappears behind the top of the hill and so you need to be well to the right of this. As you crest the hill you will see a wall (2) on either side of a metalled track.

At the wall, turn and look to your right and you will see Branch Farm. At the point where you are now there are two footpaths that cross this very large field and immediately to your front. The footpath you require is the right-hand one and nearest to the farm.

Look toward the hedge that starts at the farm-house. Follow it up to the left with your eyes to a point approximately 300 metres distant along the hedge and away from the farm. Angle slightly left and walk across the field. Pass over the stile into the next field. Walk straight across this small field that has an electric pole standing right in the middle of it. Pass to the left of it and you will see another stile.

Go over that stile and look left. There you will see a 'clump' of electric and telegraph poles. Look carefully and you will see the kissing gate. Angle left across the field to this gate (3) passing out and on to a track beyond. Immediately on the other side of the track there is another kissing gate. Pass through it and walk down the hill, passing to the left of a lovely pond that sits in front of Edney's Farm.

Walk through the fields and keep the hedges immediately on your left. You will be walking slightly uphill here. After a while you will enter a concrete works (4), passing over a stile and through a small strip of woodland. (Please keep rigidly to the well-marked footpath here, as it is a working environment and fork lift trucks are busy lifting and shifting).

About 25 metres into the concrete works you will find a little road running from left to right. Pass straight over it and again follow the well-defined footpath, keeping the hedge on your left. Pass over another small works track running left to right and into a works car park and walk towards the white Liquid Petroleum Gas tanks ahead of you.

Walk between two flat topped buildings and turn right. After about 25 metres you will need to turn left and walk past the weigh bridge, keeping to your left-hand side. Walk on out of the concrete works and up to the main road.

On the very sharp corner, turn right (5) and walk down to the old railway bridge and turn immediately right (6). Follow the sign-post that indicates National Cycle Route 24, walking down this permissive way until you come to some metal railings on your right and where the permissive way ends. Turn right on to the National Cycle Route that follows the old railway line.

On the National Cycle Route (7) turn left and follow it along towards Frome. Amazingly the old railway lines are still in existence today and stand to the left of the tarmac cycle route.

Follow this track, The Collier's Way, for about two kilometres. It boasts a veritable feast of wild life that is just waiting to be seen. Yellow Hammers, Blackbirds, Thrushes, Goldfinches and Robins were some of the birds I saw on the day I walked the line, plus such wonderful flowers as the Cow Slip and Violets, both blue and white.

This track does not allow any vehicles. It is for pedestrians, horse riders, and of course, cyclists. If you have a dog, please keep it on a lead on this track as some bicycles now travel at quite a speed and you may not hear them coming. One bonus of this flat and level tarmac track is that the disabled may access it and use their Electrically Powered Vehicles – that is allowed.

Pass under a bridge, called Jericho Bridge, and it is marked so. After a while you come across another bridge, and here you will need to walk up the paved incline (sign-posted The Talbot Inn) to the small country lane that crosses the bridge, called Conduit Bridge (8).

At the country lane, turn right and walk along it towards the church of Mells in the distance. The road now turns sharply to the left. Leave the road at this point (9) and pass through a small wall and out into the field. Angle left across the field towards the top left-hand corner where the hedges meet, passing beneath the electric lines. Pass through the gap and out into the next field, angling slightly left across it to the next stile. The church tower stands almost straight ahead of you.

Go over the stile and walk down towards the church wall. At the church wall, turn right and walk along it a little way, passing into the churchyard (10) through a gap in the wall and walking between the avenue of small evergreen trees.

At the east end of St. Andrew's Church (the end with the tower) walk across to the wall and look directly back at the church. Two people of note are buried here.

One was Lady Helen Violet Bonham-Carter, Baroness Asquith of Yarnbury, D.B.E. She was born on the 15th April 1887 and died on the 19th February 1969 and was a noted British politician and diarist. Lady Helen was also the daughter of H.H. Asquith, the British Prime Minister from 1908–1916.

Following her father's lead, she later became active in Liberal politics herself, being a leading opponent of appeasement. She became an M.P. and was eventually made a life peer. She was also involved in the arts and literature. Her published diaries cover her father's premiership before and during World War I and continued until the 1960s. She was also Winston Churchill's closest female friend, and the grandmother of the well-known actress, Helena Bonham Carter.

Behind the tombstone of this lady, and three rows back and two to the right of it, lies the grave of the famous First World War poet, Siegfried Sassoon.

Siegfried Loraine Sassoon, C.B.E., M.C. was born on the 8th September 1886 and died on the 1st September 1967. He was a famous English poet, author and soldier. Decorated for bravery on the Western Front, he became one of the leading poets of the First World War. His poetry both described the horrors of the trenches, and poked fun at the patriotic pretensions of those who, in Sassoon's view, were responsible for a vainglorious war.

One of his published poems, 'The Hero,' told the story of an officer's visit to tell a mother about the death of her son. It ended with the officer, having told the soldier's mother some untruths about the incident, mutters to himself that the man was really a coward. His brother officers were extremely angry at him for revealing such truths.

If the church is open it is well worth a visit, particularly to visit the quarter sized bronze statue of a World War One soldier, Lieutenant Edward Horner, which depicts him mounted on his horse. Lieutenant Horner had been wounded at Ypres, recuperated and returned to the Front, only to be killed there. The nursery rhyme, 'Little Jack Horner' is supposedly a true one and based on the Horner family and Mells Manor, where he lived.

Leave the church and go out of the iron gates, walking along the old-fashioned street. At the road junction (11), turn immediately right and the Talbot Inn is just there.

Monkton Combe, Somerset –
The Soldier's Walk.

Distance: approximately 5.6 kilometres.
Time: 1½ hours walking.

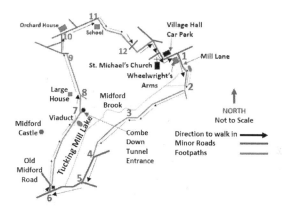

The pretty village of Monkton Combe (population about 554 in March 2011) is located some 3 miles south of Bath and about a kilometre west of the main A36 road. It has narrow streets and some wonderfully structured old buildings designed in the Bath style, but it is nestled away from the normal tourist route. The very heart of the village is dominated by the Monkton Combe School, an independent co-educational boarding and day school for pupils aged between 2 and 19 years of age.

The starting point for the walk is set on the road close to Village Hall Car Park. The map reference is ST 772 619 and the Global Positioning System co-ordinates are 51° 21' 23.07" North, 2° 19' 42.62" West. For SatNav, use the Post Code BA2 7HB.

The walk is circular but at one point becomes quite steep.   It starts at a height of 58.8 metres above sea level, and at its lowest point it is 54 metres. At its highest point the walk is about 157 metres.

The local inn is the Wheelwrights Arms. It is an old eighteenth century inn and can be found about 50 metres from the church.   The pub has an outside seating area. You can find their website at www.wheelwrightsarms.co.uk (retrieved from the web on the 8ᵗʰ January 2018) and their telephone number is 01225 722287.

Find somewhere to park near the Village Hall Car Park. Walk back down to the pub and turn immediately right into Mill Lane (1). Follow the road downhill, passing the old eighteenth century village lock up (circa 1776) with its interesting curved roof. The door has metal bars which enables the curious to peer into the heart of the lock-up, but unless you have a torch with you, its bleak interior will reveal nothing.

At the bottom of the lane the public road merges into a private one. In front of you, beneath the electricity lines, is a metal chicane. Pass through it and meander down the tarmac pavement in a generally southerly direction to the what was once the old mill race. Cross this by means of the wooden footbridge. The old mill with its weed-filled pond will be on your left.

Follow the footpath straight ahead and go over a small river by way of a humped shape wooden bridge. Take the first kissing gate (2) on your right-hand side and move out into the field beyond.

Keeping the river on your right, make your way along the bank of the pretty Midford Brook with its fast-flowing stretches supplemented by deep pools. After a while the river takes a distinct bend to the right (3) and, following the public footpath, you start gently walking uphill and moving away from it.

Keep going straight ahead and you will come to another metal kissing gate. Go through this gate and into a little wooded area. Someone has thoughtfully placed some large railway sleepers there that act as a little bridge for you to walk upon.

Very quickly you will enter an open field. Walk straight ahead and keep the wooded area and the river to your right. There is also a small wooded area on your left. Pass out of the field through a metal kissing gate and onto a small country lane (4). Behind you and across the valley stands the imposing building known as Midford Castle.

Turn right and walk on downhill. At the road junction, turn right (5) and walk along the pavement towards the old railway bridge in the distance.

You will pass a pub called the Hope and Anchor. Do not be fooled by the exterior which fronts the B3110, for its true worth will be seen shortly.

Turn right (6) into the Old Midford Road, and then cut through the pub car park to and walk up to the Route 24 National Cycle Route, the Two Tunnels Shared Route Path. Go through what was once the old Midford Station, where the opening scenes of the 1953 film, "The Titfield Thunderbolt" were taken.

Follow the tarmacadam cycle and pedestrian path along in a generally northerly direction. The old line passes beneath Midford Castle and its Church, and a fine view of it can be achieved here. After 10 minutes or so you will come to the Viaduct which crosses the valley and with a fishing pond beneath it.

The Tucking Mill Lake caters purely for disabled anglers and is maintained by Wessex Water. It offers free Coarse Fishing to them. To gain entrance as an angler, you will need to go on-line and e-mail fishing@wessexwater.co.uk with a subject line of Tucking Mill Lake. Alternatively, you could ring 0845 6004600 to try and book a space.

Pass over the large viaduct and directly in front of you is the Combe Down Tunnel. *It is 1670m in length and takes you into Bath. If you are contemplating walking through it be advised that it takes about 25 minutes to do so and will probably be considerably cooler than the day outside. The tunnel is well lit and is certainly worth a visit at some time, but probably better used from the Bath end.*

Just after the viaduct and just before the tunnel, turn left through a metal gate (7) and out into a field, turning right. Start walking uphill through an old meadow and above the tunnel. You will see a large house away to your left. At the top of the field, pass out through another metal kissing gate and onto a track that runs from left to right (8).

The walk now goes left but rises quite steeply up to the village of Combe Down. Pass by the large house you saw earlier. This will now be directly on your left. A series of steep steps will now lead you up to a small road.

Turn left (9) and almost immediately on your right, pick up the small footpath and follow it along, keeping the large stone garden wall on your left. At the top of the footpath, turn right into Belmont Road for about 5 metres until it meets another road running from your left to right. Turn right (10), ensuring that Orchard House is on your left. Head for the *"No Through Road"* sign in the distance, and when you reach it, walk through it. At the end of the road, turn right (11) on the footpath towards Monkton Preparatory School.

Walk down towards the school on the footpath, keeping the stone wall on your left. Just before the Park Swimming Centre, follow the footpath along, keeping the allotments on your left and the high chain fence of the school on your right. You now come out onto a small metalled road that runs from left to right (12). Walk straight across it and down the 50 metres or so towards a large house immediately to your front. Walk slightly to the left of the house and go through the metal kissing gate. Follow the path on down.

Exit the path and onto a small metalled road (13). Turn immediately right. We are now at a high point on the hill where someone has thoughtfully provided a wooden bench. Pause a while here to gaze across the valley, particularly at the large viaduct that carries the busy A36 from Warminster to Bath. Beneath you the village of Monkton Combe lies nestled away.

Walk down the steep and stepped footpath *(known as Drung Way)* that lies to the right of the wooden bench and follow it back down and into the village. At the junction of the path and road, walk straight ahead with the road sign 'South View' on your left. About 50 metres to your front, and on your right-hand side you will see the church.

Walk through the metal gates of the Church of St. Michael. This church with a curious tower (it almost looks as if someone has added a house to the top of it) was thought to have been originally built in Norman times but was razed to the ground in the early nineteenth century. It was rebuilt in 1814 but had significant additional works carried out on it during 1886.

Follow the footpath through the church heading towards the south west end of the churchyard. Here you will find two graves of interest, both next to the path.

The first is that of Henry John "Harry" Patch who was born on the 17th June 1898 and up until his death on the 25th July 2009, at the venerable old age of 111 years, had held the significant honour of being the last serving World War One Soldier. He was known in his later years as "the last fighting Tommy". At the time of his death he also held the unique distinction of being the third verified oldest man in the world, the oldest man in Europe and the 69th oldest man in the world.

He had been mobilised in 1916 and became an Assistant Gunner in the Lewis Gun Section of the Duke of Cornwall's Light Infantry. During the Battle of Passchendaele, he was seriously wounded by shrapnel on the 22nd September 1917.

This same shrapnel killed the other members of his team. At the Field Hospital the shard of metal was removed from his stomach, but without the use of any anaesthetic.

Surviving this terrible war, he became a successful plumber. During World War Two he became a fireman in the London Volunteer Fire Service and served in Bath, particularly at the time of the infamous "Baedeker Raids".

In 1999 he was awarded the Legion d'Honneur from the French Government and in 2008 the Knight of the Order of Leopold from Belgium.

By coincidence, next to Harry Patch there is a grave of a soldier who had survived World War Two, only to be killed in a road accident on the 10th November 1945 when the army lorry he was driving overturned.

The family gravestone marks the last resting place of Driver Edward George Mundy of the 250th (Airborne) Light Composite Company, Royal Army Service Corps.

Poor Edward had served throughout the war and had had been a paratrooper in the D-Day landings. His headstone records the fact that he was a member of the 6th

Airborne Division. The sad thing was that he was due to have been de-mobbed and was to have been returned to civilian life in the first week of December 1945.

Leave the church by the way you came in and return to your car.

Lower Weare, Somerset - The Comedians Walk.

Distance: approximately 5.5 Kilometres.

Time: 1¼ hours.

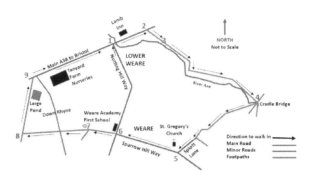

The village of Lower Weare nestles beneath the Mendip Hills and is located on the Somerset Levels. It is approximately two miles South West of Axbridge and is on the main A38 Bristol road.

The starting point for the walk can be found on Notting Hill Way (between the Lamb Inn and the Tanyard Farm Nurseries) at general Map Reference ST 405 535 and the Global Positioning co-ordinates are 51º 16'42.71" North 2º 51'11.04" West. For SatNav, use Post Code BS26 2JF. At its starting and lowest point of the walk is at 7.8 metres above sea level and rises to the highest point of about 22 metres. Most of this walk is on the flat Somerset Levels, but there is a minor hill to navigate.

Walk back from where you parked your car in Notting Hill Way towards the busy main A38 road. Turn right (1) and remain on the right-hand side of the pavement. Walk over the river by means of the road bridge. Go past the Lamb Inn on your left. Should you intend to return here for a drink or a meal later, please remember that The Lamb Inn has limited opening times, so it is worth while checking them first. Their website can be found on the internet by searching for www.thelambatweare.co.uk (retrieved from the web on the 8th January 2018) where all the details regarding opening times, food and drinks served etc. are on display. Their telephone number is 01934 732384. The pub is a local pub and frequented mostly by the local population who fondly call the place 'The Lamb at Weare.'

Walk on for about 75 metres and at the house known as 'Pear Tree Cottage' (it is pictured to the right of the pub sign), turn right (2) and walk through the parking area and out through the wooden pedestrian gate. Walk across the well-kept field that has the appearance of a lawn and head towards the top left-hand corner. At the River Axe, some 75 metres to your front, turn left (3) and pass over the stile, walking upstream. This River Axe (not to be confused with Devon's River Axe which empties out into the sea near Seaton, Devon) starts its life in the Wookey Hole cave on the Mendips. It runs through Lower Weare on its way to spill out into Weston Bay, near Uphill. In days of yore, the river was navigable from Uphill Harbour to Lower Weare and history records this.

After following the river for about 1¼ kilometres you will encounter a foot bridge (4). This bridge is known as Cradle Bridge. Cross over the River Axe by means of it.

Pass over the stile immediately to your right, angling right across the field to a point about half way along the hedge and towards the White House in the distance. Cross over another stile and footbridge and into the next field. Again, angle right and walk across the field, passing over into the next field by means of a stile and footbridge. Walk up the field with the hedge on your left and head towards the same white house you saw earlier.

Cross over into another small field and through the metal gate on your left, angling slightly right and keeping the small pond to your left. The path goes through the grounds of the house immediately to your front. Pass slightly to the right of the garage and walk on up the drive (Splott Lane) to the road junction ahead.

Turn right (5) and walk along the raised church path opposite the house named 'Cops Cottage'. Be warned; if you have children running ahead of you, you will need to keep tight control of them at this point as there are no railings to safeguard them from the high drop on to the road below, although there is a very low stone wall offering some sort of protection.

On reaching the graveyard the church will be directly in front of you. To your right is a wall, and behind that wall is the newer graveyard extension. Pass through to it. To your right and towards the far end of the churchyard extension you will see a pink coloured granite slab in the second row out from the wall. This marks the final resting place of Francis Alick Howard, OBE.

His stage name was Frankie Howerd, and he was well known for his acting roles in such films as the 'Carry On' series and the television series of thirteen episodes, each of thirty minutes duration, 'Up Pompeii,' where he played the part of the tongue-in-cheek slave, Lercio. This series was first broadcast between 1969 and 1970. In the row just behind him lies his partner of 40 years.

Pass out of the churchyard through the metal gates by the church tower and walk along the road in a generally north-westerly direction until you come to the

"T" junction. The village school, Weare Academy First School, (6) is ahead of you and there is a road sign saying: 'Notting Hill Way' ahead of you.

To the left of the school there is a track. Cross over the road and on to this track, passing over a wooden stile. Walk up along the well-marked track and keep the ditch and hedge to your right.

After a while, the track bends to the left. Ignore this bend and keep walking alongside the hedge until you reach a large willow tree to your front. There will be a few apple trees to your left. Pass through a metal gate and into the field, turning immediately left. Walk up the field, keeping the hedge on your left and a well-defined circular area of scrubland on (7) your right.

You now cross over another bridge. Beneath it runs one of the famous Rhyne's of the Somerset Level. This deep and shallow clear running stream is known as "Down Rhyne".

Angle slightly left across the field towards the hedge in the distance, and for the first time you start to walk uphill, but not too steeply. At the bridge the height is 10 metres above sea level and as you walk up the hill you will reach its highest point of some 22 metres. Do not go through the stile (8) to your front but turn right here and walk on down the hill towards the large greenhouses in the distance, aiming for a point in the hedge just a little to the left of halfway along the hedge. Look out carefully for the stile here, as it passes through a thick hedge and is well disguised until you reach that point.

Walk straight across the field to your front, passing over a foot bridge that takes you across another Rhyne. Walk straight across the field towards the metal gate ahead of you and to the left of the greenhouses. As you walk across the field you will pass a large and square pond on your right. Pass through the metal gate and out onto the main A38 Bridgwater to Bristol road (9). Turn right, with the Tanyard Farm Nurseries on your right. Cross over the main road and follow the paved pedestrian foot-path back to your car.

Ilchester, Somerset –
The Legionnaire's March.

Distance: approximately 12 kilometres.
Time: 2½ hours.

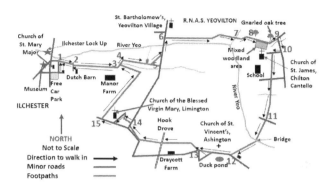

The village of Ilchester (population 2,153 in March 2011) was known in Roman times as Lendinis and is snuggled in behind the junction where the A37 meets the A303 and located about 5 miles north of Yeovil, Somerset.

The starting point for the walk is in the free car between Church Street and Limington Road.   It is located at Grid Reference ST 522 225 and its Global Positioning co-ordinates are 51° 00' 01.28" North and 2° 40' 54.27" West. For SatNav, use Post Code BA22 8LW. At its beginning the walk is 20 metres above sea level, and at its lowest point is just 9 metres. It rises to a highest point of about 28 metres. The walk follows the flood plains of the River Yeo.

Walk out of the car park and cross the road into Free Street, keeping the little house "Tolouse Chaumiere" on your left.   After approximately 100 metres the road bends sharply to the left, but you need to go straight ahead and go over the clearly visible stone steps. At the bottom of the steps (1) go through a metal kissing gate and out into a field. The River Yeo will be on your left-hand side.

Walk diagonally left across the first field, keeping the hedge close to you and walk on through another metal kissing gate. Keep walking and you will cross over a small stream by means of a stone footbridge. Still keep the hedge on your left and walk ahead. Cross over a farm track, keeping the near-by Dutch barn on your right-hand side.

Head up the small hill (2) towards the top left-hand corner of the hedge in front of you (R.N.A.S. Yeovilton will come into view as you go down this slope). Once there, keep the hedge on your right and follow it down, crossing into another field by means of a stile. Follow the well-defined path and exit out of a metal gate. Keep Manor Farm on your right.

At this gate, bear sharp left (3) to the small concrete bridge that spans the mill stream and cross over (4) it. If you approach this area quietly you may be rewarded with the sight of feeding Herons or the unmistakeable white Egrets which are just starting to populate this area. Follow the mill stream along, keeping it to your right, and go over another small concrete bridge, with another stream running off to your left.

Go over the field ahead and through the next gate. There you will find a wooden footbridge crossing this small stream on your right-hand side. Ignore this.

Angle left (5) across the field, heading for the metal road gate away in the distance to your front and for the right-hand side of the Ilchester Weir road bridge. Cross this river bridge into Yeovilton village. At the very first house on the right-hand side you will notice a Footpath sign that points the way to "BRIDGEHAMPTON 2 miles". This is the Footpath that we (6) want.

Before following this foot-path you may wish to consider visiting the Church of St Bartholomew which is about 500 metres further up into the village. The church belongs to the Fleet Air Arm and is known affectionately by service personnel as St. Bart's.

The metal gates of the porch of the church entrance are emblazoned with two golden coloured Fleet Air Arm emblems. The Church is open by appointment only. Please call 01935 455257 or email navyyeo-chaplaincyshared@mod.uk should you wish to look inside the church.

There is a Royal Naval burial plot to the east of the church, with Second World War burials to the church's front and left-hand side as you look at it from the road. It is a peaceful and serene area and is a place where one can be alone with their thoughts. Gazing at the headstones of these men and women you quickly realise that there is an ultimate price to be paid, and not always in war.

Return to the weir and pick up the footpath sign for Bridgehampton that will appear on your left, slightly hidden by the last house before the weir. Keeping the River Yeo to your right, go straight across the field along the well-marked footpath through horse paddocks and pass through the pedestrian gates. Head towards the far right-hand corner of the field where the hedge meets the river. There will be a small footbridge on your right-hand side crossing the River Yeo. Ignore this bridge.

Once more, go through a gate. Now, keeping the hedge immediately on your left, walk up towards R.N.A.S. Yeovilton. Keep the security fence on your left-hand side. At the far end of the field you will see some iron gates that are permanently closed so that you can go no further. Cross the stream by the (7) footbridge and go into the next field by use of another small footbridge that crosses a very deep ditch.

Keeping the river on your right, head across the field towards a large Ash tree in the far distance, to the right of an Oak tree and a ruined building that stands in a clump of (8) greenery on the left. Keep the river on your immediate right until you come to the next pedestrian metal gateway.

Across the field there is a small square of shrub and trees. Head for the left-hand edge of this, keeping the fence on your left and the single oak tree in the field to the right.

Pass through a metal pedestrian gate, and with the small wooded area on your right, follow the well-trodden pathway to the end. You will then pass through another metal gate and out into another field.

Head straight across this field towards the metal gate in the distance, passing a magnificent and gnarled old oak tree on your left. Keep slightly to the left of the large building that lies towards your front. Exit out of the field (9) on to a minor road.

Turn immediately right on this road and pass over the small river bridge to the next crossroads. Turn right into the village of Chilton Cantello (10) where it is sign-posted.

Just before the church of St James's, turn left on to the footpath. The footpath is sign-posted "ASHINGTON 1m". Follow this easily identifiable footpath. After approximately 300m you will cross over a small road which leads directly into the school car-park, with large lumps of ham-stone placed strategically on the grass to stop illicit vehicle parking. Cross over and head in a generally south-west direction along the well-defined track to your front. Pass over a small stream by means of a concrete bridge and keeping walking ahead.

You will shortly come to a metalled road. Turn immediately right (11) and, keeping the garden wall on your left-hand side, after about 10 metres, turn left on to another well-defined footpath. The footpath is sign-posted "ASHINGTON ¾ m" and follows the line of the hedge.

At the end of this well-marked track, cross over a small footbridge into the field. In front of you are a line of electric poles. Head at a slightly left angle away from these poles and walk towards a pedestrian gate which is at the river and slightly left of the hedge that runs down towards you. Cross the River Yeo by the iron footbridge.

Follow the edge of the field, keeping the hedge close to your right-hand side. At the very top of the field pass out through the gate to the right of the left-hand house and onto the metalled road, turning right (12) into Ashington.

In Ashington you will pass between a duck pond and the small Church of St. Vincent. The church does not have a tower, but it does have an unusual bell housing.

Keeping to the right-hand side of the road, and just after the church, there is a footpath signpost that states "LIMINGTON 1m". Go through the gate and though the horse paddocks, exiting by means of the gates. Head towards the hedge to your front, keeping the trees on your left and the red house just on your right. Go through the metal pedestrian gate and down the steps to re-join the road.

On the road, turn right and walk for about 75m, and enter a field through another metal pedestrian gate on (13) your right. The footpath is sign-posted. Angle left across the field and over a footbridge that lies about 100 metres up from the red house. Look up towards the electric poles in front of you, and head for the one just to the right of the hedge that comes up from the red house. Once there, pass underneath the electric line and keep the next hedge immediately on your left. Follow it along.

You will then need to angle right towards a pair of white houses in the distance but keeping them to your left as you head towards the far hedge that hides a sunken track that is named Hook Drove. You get on to this track by a small wooden footbridge that crosses the ditch and you will see a stile immediately in front of you.

Go over this stile and head towards the telegraph pole in the middle of the field. Keep to the right of this telegraph pole and walk towards the double stile in the hedge to your front.

Angle to the right of the left-hand corner edge of the fence you have just crossed. Cross the large ditch by means of a footbridge, keeping the fence and farm buildings to the left. Cross over the next stile in front of you and head to the right of the white house's we spoke about earlier. Pass through another stile in front of this house and angle right across the field, keeping the farm buildings on your left. Go over a stile and out onto a (14) metalled road.

Turn right and walk on for about 10 metres. Go left over a stile into a field, and angle towards the top right-hand corner of the small field. Go out through a pedestrian "V" and turn right into the churchyard. Then turn immediately left, walking past two young Yew trees on your left.

Go out through the Church gate and on to the metalled road. Turn right and follow the road around the sharp left-hand turn. After about 150 metres you will cross over a small stream that runs beneath the road. Turn right (15) opposite the grey-stoned house called "Hillview" and go through two metal pedestrian gates that lead through a field. Go out into the second field and walk down to the mill stream. Turn left here and follow it along until you come the concrete bridge you crossed earlier in the walk. Go left and retrace your steps (3) along the footpath that you have previously passed over and return to Ilchester and your car.

Go over the stone steps and turn right, following the road down. At the main road, turn right and cross over to the pavement on the over side of the road. Where the bridge over the River Yeo widens in the centre, turn around and look back into Ilchester.

In the very small promontory on your right you can still visualise the small-town gaol that stood there in 1540. About 50 metres from there and to your front would have been the walled town of Ilchester, with one of the main gates directly in front of you.

Turn around, and where the bridge ends and to the left of the garage stood the notorious Ilchester Goal. It stood on that site from 1599 until it was closed in 1843.

Walk back into the town and you will find the market cross in front of you. Cross over the road into the High Street and just past the Town Hall you will find the Ilchester Museum. There is an old Mile Stone just by the museum that is worth looking at. The Museum is open for business from Easter Saturday until the end of September. It also opens on a Thursday and a Saturday from 10 a.m. until 4 p.m. and entrance is free (retrieved from the web on the 17th November 2017).

It is worth paying a visit to the museum, as the town is a place steeped in history. Exhibits from the remains of the notorious Ilchester Gaol can be seen here, together with Roman and other artefacts. There is also a permanent window display showing some of the things that have been found in the village that can be observed even when the museum is closed.

Retrace your steps and you will be in Church Street. The Ilchester Arms will be across the road from you. Walk back along the footpath until you come the to the church of St. Mary Major.

If it is open it is indeed worth a visit. Inside you will find a plaque commemorating one of the town's most famous sons, Roger Bacon, the noted Franciscan monk, mathematician, optician and scholar. Installed within the Church is a brass plaque which relates his achievements and records that he was born in Ilchester in 1214 and died in Oxford in 1294.

Haselbury Plucknett, Somerset –
The Anchorite Priest's Walk.

Distance: approximately 4.2 kilometres.
Time: 1 hour.

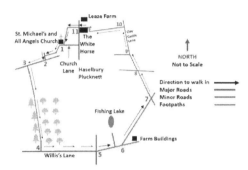

Haselbury Plucknett (population about 411 in March 2011) is a small village that that can be found south of the A30 between Yeovil and Crewkerne and straddles the A3066. The village is located at Map Reference ST 472 109 and Global Positioning Position coordinates 50° 53' 45.0" North, 2° 45' 05.77" West. For SatNav, use Post Code TA18 7RE. The walk passes over level pastureland and minor roads. Its starting and lowest point is about 39 metres above sea level and at its highest point is 70.2 metres.

G o past the White Horse Inn and just before the school, turn right into Church Lane. Find somewhere to park by the church.

Enter the Church of St Michaels. Here the anchorite priest Wulfric is secretly buried. He lived in a monk's cell adjacent to the current Church for about 29 years. When he died in his cell on the 20th February 1154 he had been visited frequently by two reigning monarchs of the time, Henry 1st and Stephen. It was said that he had received the gifts of prophecy and healing and had taken part in many miraculous events. On the north wall of the church, approximately near where his cell was once located, there is a large notice board on display which details his full history.

On his death Wulfric was buried in his cell by Robert of Lewes, the first Bishop of Bath and Wells. To prevent the saint's bones from being pilfered, the priest

Osbern moved Wulfric's remains twice. They ended up somewhere in the west end of the church in a position known only to him.

Within the Church there are three modern style stained glass windows which are well worth a look. Each window has its own title, Resurrection, Transfiguration, and Birth.

Go out of the church and head towards the road. Leave the churchyard and walk straight up the track to your front for about 20 metres. Pick up the footpath sign on your left, keeping the church (1) to your rear.

Follow the well-defined footpath along. Ignore the path to your left that is marked by two large and upright stones that appears after a short way. Keep walking ahead and soon you will come to a little lane. Turn left and walk the few metres to the road.

Turn right (2) and walk about 120 metres up the road until you see a sign-post on the wall which reads "Swan Hill". Cross the road here and pick up the sign opposite that indicates 'North Perrott 1 mile'.

Walk up the concrete driveway (3) for a little way and go through a kissing gate out into the field beyond. Head straight across the field towards the high trees to your front, passing through another kissing gate. Keeping the trees on your right and the apple orchard on the left, follow the trees along on to what will soon become a restricted byway with trees on both sides.

At the end of the byway you will walk out on to a metalled road (4) which is called Willis's Lane. Turn left and follow the minor road along. You will pass the North Perrott Cricket Ground on your right.

At the crossroads (5) walk straight over the A3066 and into the lane beyond, keeping the North Perrott Farm Shop and Garden Centre on your left. Walk up the metalled lane (another restricted Byway) and head up towards the Water Meadow Lakes and Lodges, passing these on your left.

In front of you and further along the way are some farm buildings. Just before you reach them, climb over the stile on your left (6) and cross the small field and go over another stile. Angle right towards the metal gate in the distance. Go over the stile next to this gate and angle left towards the gate with the large Oak tree behind it. Keep the houses in the distance to your right.

Pass out of the field through a small pedestrian gate and over a well-defined farm track (7). Go over this track and pass through the metal gate in the hedge and out into the field. Turn immediately left, and, keeping the hedge on your left, follow it all the way down the long field until you come to a metal gate. Go over the stile and onto the metalled road ahead.

At this road "T" junction, walk straight over the triangular shaped (8) ground which bears a standard road sign, following the road ahead and passing through the national road limit "30" miles per hour road signs towards the Dutch Barn which lies to the right.

Walk up the lane and just after "Pump Cottage" which you will find on your left, take the next turning right (9) into Clay Castle Lane (not sign-posted). Follow this road along until you see a small clump of trees on your left. Unusually the footpath sign is set out in the lane and on the grass verge.

Turn left here (10) and go through the metal kissing gate and out into the field beyond. Keeping the hedge on the left, follow it along all the way through the long field with the electric lines on your right. There is a plainly visible farm that is over on your right.

At the end of the field, turn right. Just before the farm, pass through another metal kissing gate on your left. Walk over the old stone bridge that crosses the gurgling brook and follow the little lane along until you come to the White Horse public house.

The White Horse has set hours that it is open so if you are planning to use it you are advised to telephone 01460 78873. It also cooks home produced meals and is website can be found at www.thewhitehorsehaselbury.co.uk (retrieved from the web on the 8th January 2018).

Leave the White Horse and walk immediately across the road (11) and through the metal gate. Walk towards the churchyard beyond keeping the hedge on your left-hand side. When you reach the churchyard wall, turn left down the well-defined path and return to Church Street. Return to your car.

Dowlish Wake, Somerset –
The Explorer's Walk.

Distance: approximately 2.56 kilometres.
Time: 50 minutes walking.

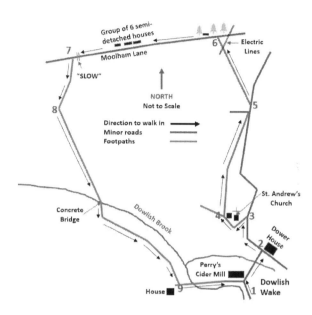

Dowlish Wake (population about 277) is one of those small and utterly charming and picturesque villages that Somerset is rightly renowned for. This short walk takes you through a world of thatched cottages, a cider farm, a babbling brook running through the centre of the village with a medieval pack bridge, holly hocks and a countryside environment that can be easily found just 2 miles south of Ilminster and 5 miles north-east of Chard, South Somerset.

The village is located at Map Reference ST 375 128 and Global Positioning System co-ordinates 50° 54'37.16" North, 2° 53'22.27" West. For SatNav, use Post Code TA19 0NY.

The walk is circular and passes over pastureland and minor roads. It starts at an elevation of 61 metres above sea level and at its lowest point is 52.7 metres. The highest point of the walk reaches 91 metres.

Find somewhere to park safely near the Perry's Cider Farm in the (1) village centre. Curb your curiosity to visit it, for we shall be finishing the walk there. Walk on up the road until you come across an unexpectedly delightful and unusual 17th century pack horse bridge on your left.

Take your time to stroll over the bridge and peer down into the clear waters of the shallow stream that gently bubbles beneath. During very wet weather this little brook can become a raging torrent as the water cascades across the road and under the four arches. Be careful if you have small children with you, for the ramparts on each side of the bridge are less than a foot in height.

Having crossed the bridge, follow the road around to your left. On your right-hand side there is a road sign-post that points you in the direction of "Kingstone, ½ mile". You need to walk that way (2), but before you do take notice of the house that stands directly in front of you. It is known as the Dower House. It dates from 1664 and at one stage was leased to female members of the locally well-known Speke family, hence its name.

Keep walking up the road and follow the rising foot path that leads you towards the ham stone Norman church of St Andrew. Go through the metal gates opposite the ham-stone village war memorial and enter the churchyard (3). In the north-east corner of the church, and to the right of a stained-glass window dedicated to John Hanning Speke, you will find a beautifully polished raised black marble sarcophagus that contains the mortal remains of that famous soldier and explorer. Around the edge of the coffin is inscribed: "John Hanning, second son of William and Georgina Speke who died September 15[th,] 1864."

Together with a fellow explorer, Richard Burton, the pair set off to explore Lake Tanganyika and whilst in Africa they heard rumours about another great lake. The two men decided that Speke would go on alone to investigate this and it was he who discovered and named Lake Victoria. He also held the strong conviction that this was the source of the Nile. The two men fell out and this led to bitter recriminations between them for the rest of their lives.

Speke returned to Africa with another expedition and eventually, on the 28th July 1862, he stood beside the falls and very close to the spot where the famous River Nile flows out of the lake. By land and river, Speke followed the river down to Cairo before returning to England to report his findings to the Royal Geographical Society.

The day before he was due to have a public debate in Bath, Somerset, with Burton, Speke was climbing over a wall in the pursuit of partridge shooting near his uncle's house in Neston Park, Wiltshire. Somehow the gun he was carrying accidentally went off and he was shot. Poor John then bled to death.

Leave the church and return out through the metal gates. Turn right, passing through the church car park and keeping the church wall on your right. Ahead of you is the Church Hall.

To the left of this hall, pass out through a metal 'V' gate into the (4) field beyond. Keeping the hedge directly on your right, walk uphill and follow it along. Just before the field ends, pass out of a large gap into the small country lane

Turn left here and follow the little lane along for a little while until you come to a farm track that bears away to your left. On the very bend of the road and just in front of this track, pick up the footpath sign and pass through the gap into the field (5).

Walk diagonally right across this field towards the far corner. Large conifer trees lie prominently behind the hedge. Pass beneath some electrical wires and walk out of the field into Moolham Lane (6). Turn left and follow the road along on the right-hand side, facing the oncoming traffic.

After a while you will come across a track (7) which is marked by a footpath sign and just before a large marking of **SLOW** painted in white upon the road. Turn left here and follow the track down and out into a field beyond (8) with a good view across the little valley.

Look down towards the stream where you can see Alder trees growing, and with your eyes, follow it along to the left until it meets a prominent ditch that could be mistaken for a hedge (see point of red arrow). Another hedge across the river will be running down to meet this ditch. Angle right across this field and contour down the slope and through a gap to a small river known as Dowlish Brook which will be flowing from left to right.

Cross over the brook by the concrete bridge and out into the field. Angle left across the field, keeping the far hedge on your right and heading just slightly left of the right-hand corner of the field. Pass through the metal pedestrian gate and out into the next field.

Follow the footpath along towards the far hedge and move towards the far metal gate, keeping it to your left. The field considerably narrows at this point. Pass through another metal pedestrian gate and out into a narrow field.

Walk towards the left-hand corner of this field, keeping the large house in the distance to your right. The field gradually peters out into a small track that leads on to another track. Pass though the metal gate and turn left (9).

Follow this track which over the brook by means of a raised pathway and wooden bridge. Soon you will arrive at the Perry's Cider Mill, complete with its own spacious car park.

Cider is still produced here, and it is open for all to visit. There is also a little museum within the complex that reflects the history of cider.

An old barn has been converted into a large tea room and eatery, together with a farm shop. Behind the counter there are several large wooden barrels of the Mill's world-famous product - cider. To the right of the counter there are some more wooden barrels with small plastic sample cups conveniently placed there. You are welcome to taste one of their many varieties of cider they have on sale. The Mill has its own website at www.perryscider.co.uk (retrieved from the web on the 8th January 2018) and that will give you fuller information about it. There are toilet facilities here.

Leave the Cider Mill and turn immediately left. Return to your car.

West Coker, Somerset -
"George's Walk".

Distance: approximately 5.5 kilometres.
Time: 1½ hours.

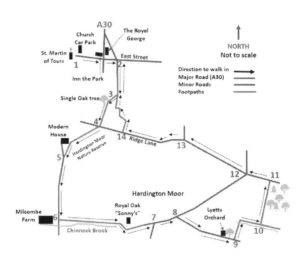

West Coker is a large village (population 2,018 in March 2011) situated some 4.8 km south west of Yeovil in the South Somerset district. The village is located at Map Reference ST 516 135 and Global Positioning System co-ordinates 50° 55'11.34" North, 2° 41' 19.32" West. For SatNav, use Post Code BA22 9BD (this will take you to the Inn the Square).

If you are arriving on the A30 main road from the direction of Yeovil, turn right at the traffic lights in the village and go into Church Road. There is a car park at the end of the road and next to the Church. Next to the car park and in the grounds of the Old Rectory there is a magnificent specimen of an evergreen tree called the Wellingtonian (Sequoiadendron giganteum) tree, although the plaque beneath calls it a "Wellington" tree.

The walk is saucepan shaped and passes over a high ridge, through a nature reserve, pastureland and minor roads. It starts at an elevation of 80 metres above sea level and at its lowest point is 53 metres. At its highest point the walk reaches 132 metres.

I have named this walk after a certain Golden Retriever dog that is a good friend of mine and frequents the Pen Mill Hotel in Yeovil, Somerset. He has an unusual passion for water and Chinnock Brook is just what he wags his tail about.

The Church of St. Martin of Tours (usually open between 9 a.m. and 4 p.m., but not always), is well worth a visit. There has been a church there since the 13th century but most of the current Church was rebuilt and added on to between 1863 and 1864.

In the tower turret there are three windows that are best viewed from outside the Church. The bottom one is made of ancient glass whilst the two above are made from cow's horn. The common usage in the 14th century for this material was to make reflectors out of translucent sheets of horn and these were named Lanthorns. From this ancient word the current usage equivalent is Lantern.

Inside the Church and in the Lady Chapel part, and to the left of the aisle, there is the beautiful Portman Memorial which remembers Sir John's daughters, Elizabeth Portman (1593-1603) and Grace Portman (1601-1611). The full history of the memorial is written there.

Leave the church (1) and walk down to the traffic lights, with the "Inn the Square" on your left. Its website can be found at innthesquare.co.uk. If would wish to have a meal, the opening times can easily be checked on this site.

Walk across the road and into East Street with the Post Office to your front. Follow the road along until just before Manor Street and you see a footpath sign for Ridge Lane on your right that leads into East Close. Walk up this lane (2) and through the metal kissing gate into the first field.

Walking steeply uphill, keep the hedge immediately on your right. Just before the Oak trees away to your right, go through a metal gate (3) and out into the next field, angling left towards the single Oak tree for about a distance of 20 metres, cutting off the corner of the field. Go through the gap in the hedge and into the next field.

Keeping the bank with the Oak Trees immediately on your right, follow it up and leave the field by the gate on to a metalled road. Cross straight over this road and through a kissing gate and enter the (4) Hardington Moor National Nature Reserve. There are some boards here which show a map of the Reserve with an explanation of what grows there.

Angle right and down over the hill across the field, keeping the hedge on your left. Pass through the gateway into the next field beyond. Keeping the house in front of you to your right, angle across this field and through the gateway. There is a wooden bench here dedicated to the memory of 'Bill Laughlin's Unquenchable Spirit'.

Walk down the hill towards the unmistakeably ultra-modern designed house and go by it, keeping it to your right. Pass beneath the electric lines which cross the field and at the end of the field go out through the kissing gate into a metalled lane (5). Turn left and follow it all the way downhill to the stream called Chinnock Brook.

On your left-hand side will be the Hardington Community Field. Just before the small bridge, turn left (6) and follow the well-marked path. Keep the stream on your right. This track leads into a metalled lane.

Follow this lane, with houses and bungalows on each side of you, until you come to The Royal Oak public house on your left.

This pub is known locally as 'Sonny's' and is sometimes frequented by motorcycle enthusiasts. Bike models such as Harley Davidsons, Gold Wings and many other types or rare and vintage machines often make an appearance, especially on sunny weekends. If you do go in there, the mural on the wall of the skittle alley is well worth a good look and reflects an almost bygone era.

At the T-junction by the pub's signpost, turn left (7) towards Yeovil. Follow the road for a short distance to the next signpost that says "Lyatts ¼ M". Turn right here (8) and walk down the lane. After the first group of houses on your left there is a small orchard within the gardens of a house called "Lyatts Orchard". Just past here pick up the footpath sign for "Primrose Hill" and turn left (9) into the orchard over the stile. Keeping the wooden fence on your left-hand side, crossing over a small stream by a footbridge and out into the next field.

Angle right across the field, keeping the stream on your right. Go over the stile next to the metal gate and out into the next field. Keep the stream (although it looks more like a ditch by now) on your right. About 50 metres later you will join another footpath that goes right over a small footbridge and into the next field. Ignore this footbridge, but turn immediately left (10), going straight across the field to the far stile (there is a large house in a noticeably wooded area just to the right of it). Cross over the stile and onto a track, keeping the high fence on your right.

Walk up the lane until you get to a tarmacadam lane. A sign on your left shows that you are now on a bridleway and points towards Primrose Hill. Turn left (11) and walk down to the crossroads on the minor road. Go straight across (12), following the road signpost for West Coker. After about 250 metres, bear left at the first T-junction (13) you come to. You are now walking along the ridge way with sweeping views across the valley to Hardington Mandeville on your left and Yeovil to your right.

After a while you will come to a very sharp right-hand bend in an otherwise straight road. Just after the bend turns sharply away to the left you will find a gate on your right-hand side with a well-marked (14) track. Go through this gate, keeping the hedge on your left-hand side. Walk on down over the hill and you will soon see that this was the field you entered in the first place.

Follow the footpath down and back to your car. If you are thirsty, you will find two pubs quite close to each other. One is called Inn the Square whilst the other, to the right of the traffic lights, is The Royal George.

Stoke-sub-Hamdon, Somerset -
The Dog Lover's Walk.

Distance: approximately 5.7 kilometres.
Time: 1½ hours.

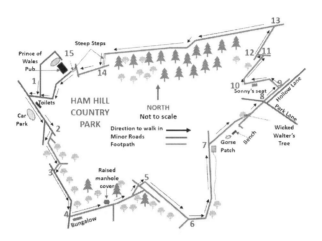

The village of Stoke sub Hamdon (population 1,969 in March 2011) lies just west of Yeovil and off the main A303 trunk road between Yeovil and Ilminster. Find somewhere to park near the Prince of Wales pubic house. It can be found at Grid Reference ST 479 168, Global Positioning System co-ordinates 50° 56' 55.10" North, 2° 44' 34.14" West. For SatNav, use Post Code TA14 6RW to bring you near to the pub.

The Prince of Wales Public House is a favourite amongst dog walkers due to its location and beautiful countryside surrounding the hill. It is also a dog friendly pub. Full details can be found on their website, www.princeofwaleshamhill.co.uk

The walk is circular and starts at the top of the hill. It goes along the top of the old Roman hill fort and is fairly level until a deep descent takes place. It starts at an elevation of 120 metres above sea level and at its lowest point is 49 metres. At its highest it is 121 metres. The walk does follow so well-worn tracks, and for this reason the walk is best taken during the spring or summer months, or after a prolonged spell of dry weather. Ham Hill is a large source of water and most of it seeps out and across the tracks, particularly during the last part of the walk, so can be very muddy.

L eave your car (1) and walk back to the minor road, turning left and walking along it. You will soon pass a lay-by on your right that has panoramic views across the Somerset countryside. A Hawk regularly hunts here, and you may be lucky enough to find it hovering just in front of you, holding itself almost motionless in the wind as it rides its wild current.

Walk on along this road, passing the road junction that goes steeply downhill to the right. About 75 metres from this turning go right and on to the footpath (2). It is sign-posted "Little Norton/Norton sub Hamdon". Walk along the path for a few metres and take the right-hand path that is sign-posted "Friends Path/Jack "O" Beards Bench" and follow it down the hill until you come across "Jack O' Beards" metal bench. Go right here, keeping the bench on your left, and join the metalled road.

Turn left (3), following the road downhill. At the distinct right-hand bend, go through the national 30 m.p.h. speed limit signs, and just slightly past them turn left (4) up the concrete driveway and follow the signpost that indicates "Norton's Covert ½". After about 20 metres, and just before the bungalow, bear left up the track and through a gate on to a footpath.

Neat piles of kindling are stacked everyone, and the almost lost art of coppicing is much in evidence. The hazel trees are generally surrounded by round fences of interwoven branches and twigs, just the thing to stop the hungry deer for grazing upon them.

Follow the track all the way through the wood. The field to your right is an orchard. You will then come to the first obvious T-junction that lies just beyond a raised and round concrete manhole with a metal inspection cover. Take the left-hand track that goes uphill.

Shortly, and on your right-hand side, you will notice the buildings which proclaim the Tinker's Bubble camp. The residents here enjoy an alternative life style, so, please respect their privacy.

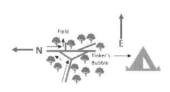

There are several tracks that converge at this point, with a triangle of grass and shrubs that separates them. Go left, then immediately right, taking the direction of the foot-path sign that records "Little Norton ½". Walk down over the steep bank and out through the wooden gate into the field beyond. In front of you is a beautiful valley which we will be passing through shortly.

Turn right (5). Walk down the field keeping the wood immediately on your right. There is a track that runs parallel to you within the wood, but it is mostly sunken and hides the wonderful vista that now unfolds in front of you.

At the end of the field, turn left (6) at the footpath sign "Witcombe Lane ¾". Walk across the field to the wood to your front. Turn left, walking straight up the hill and keeping the first mixed wood (with a large farm type building) on your right.

Where the wood goes off to your right, walk straight on up the hill towards a clump of willow trees to your front.

Keep the ditch with its watering points on your right. You should now be walking up the valley re-entrant, with the tinker's hollow campsite in the wood directly on your left-hand side. Walk on up the valley and you will see a fenced off pond on your right.

Walk just beyond this pond. The well-marked track goes straight ahead and to the right of the house in the distance, but you need to angle right uphill (7) and go along the tractor-wheeled track to the hedge on the horizon to your right. A patch of gorse high on the hill to your right and, to the left of it, a metal bench, confirms that you are on the right track. When you reach the hedge, turn left and walk along it, keeping the farm track on your right-hand side.

Glance back down to the valley and you will identify patches of stinging nettles and ridges that indicate that once the medieval village of Witcombe was there. Nettles were a mainstay food in medieval times and what is left of these vegetable patches, together with lumps and ridges in the ground, are all that remains of the village which seems to have disappeared around about 1566.

There is a story that the wicked elf, Walter of Witcombe, cast a spell upon the village when some of the local children threw stones at him. In retribution he banished the village from the earth. Is this a true story? I do not know, but soon you will come across an old oak tree on your right that has had its main branches cut off to help it to keep upright during very windy days. At the base of this tree is supposedly where Wicked Walter lived, although the wooden panelled front door appears to be now firmly locked.

Follow the track along until you come to a pedestal which details the history of Witcombe. Turn right here and out through a wooden gate on to the track proper. Turn left through another gate and this will lead you out on to a metalled road.

Cross over this road (8) and go towards the metal gate opposite just at the beginning of the road called "Hollow Lane". Just to the right of the steel gate is a pedestrian gate. Go through it and keep walking to the top of the field along the obvious trackway. At the next footpath gate turn left (9), keeping the far cluster of buildings to your left and follow the path along. Ignore any tracks that go down to the right.

Bear left through another footpath gate and soon you will pass beneath some electric wires. Pause for a while on the metal resting place that you will come across that bears the legend "Sonny's Seat". Relax and study the beautiful scene which has unfolded before you – the church, the tower and the imposing structure of Abbey Farm (which all are down in the valley). Buzzards often use the updraft from this hill to soar into the sky above, and you may be lucky enough to see one or two.

When you are ready, walk on for another few metres and go through a footpath gate. Turn right (10) and will now start walking downhill. Follow the track down to the bottom. In front of you and on the far side of the field there is a wood. Turn right and follow the stone wall along, keeping the wood away to the left. Where the stone wall almost meets the edge of the wood, go through the footpath gate and into the field (11) beyond.

Turn immediately left and go over the stile into the wood. About 50 metres later you will meet another track crossing in front of you. Turn right. (12). Follow this bridle way until you get to the next track junction with a field to your front. Turn left (13) and follow it along for about 1.2 kilometres. Ignore any other turnings to your left or right and walk along until you come to a set of (14) steep steps. Walk up them and bear right along the track.

As you near the end of the trail you will observe the Prince of Wales public house above you and to your front. Follow the track back to it, keeping the field on your right. Climb the steep set of ham-stone steps (15) that lead you up to the front of the pub and back to where you left your car.

INDEX

Printed in Great Britain
by Amazon